T0383188

Endorsements

If you are a Change Leader or simply interested in the topic, this is a must read. Make sure to buy a copy of *Leading Business Change*. It is one of the few books that I have already read twice. I have a lot of faith in Karin Stumpf's book as it is written based on her previous experience working for some of the top-notch consulting companies this planet has to offer.

Navid Nazemian

Global HR Business Partner at Roche, Switzerland, and University Lecturer

This book is based on Karin's common sense paired with her vast experiences in supporting organizations with their change processes. In fact, it's an easy-to-read forceful resource and it's useful for all those dealing with change in an organization.

Roberto Wittlin

Head PMO Services and Change Management at AXA Winterthur

Karin Stumpf has captured the challenges and the trade-offs integral to today's dynamic organizational changes. She also presents solutions which are, in general, broadly applicable, but go much beyond the mere mundane and the cookie cutter recipes.

Sam N. Basu

Professor of Economics, Finance and Global Business
Cotsakos College of Business
William Paterson University

Leading Business Change is an excellent book for people managers and leaders who want to understand how the theory applies in everyday life when dealing with change management challenges. It saves you a lot of "trial and error" mistakes and therefore truly boosts your transformation process and your development towards a true Change Master.

Luca Bitonto

Head of Learning and Organizational
Development, eBay

There's no question that the ability to promote and manage change in your organization is a leadership requirement for today's fast-paced, global economy. In her book *Leading Business Change: A Practical Guide to Transforming Your Organization* Dr. Karin Stumpf shows leaders not only how they can enable their employees to commit to change, but how leaders can encourage their employees to feel a sense of shared ownership in driving that change forward.

Tanveer Naseer

Leadership Coach, Speaker and Writer

Dr. Stumpf has created a nice, easy-to-remember change model from her real-world organizational experiences. She will show you three phases in the change process—how to mobilize, crusade, and populate—so that you can lead change successfully in your organization. In today's world, one needs to be a Change Master in order to keep up. Dr. Stumpf's book will help you move in that direction.

James G. Clawson

Johnson & Higgins Professor of Business
The Darden School, University of Virginia

Business leaders and change practitioners will certainly benefit from Karin's approach to organizational change. She draws a meaningful picture of today's leadership challenges, and proposes a simple and practical framework to address the impact of the human and organizational reactions during change initiatives.

Carole Levesque

Director, Change Management and Organizational
Transformation, Bombardier Aerospace

Because I am a former aviation fighter pilot, converted into a management researcher, the book and the position of Karin Stumpf spoke to me. To continue the maritime analogy of the author, I would say that when situations of change or mergers arise, managers always fantasize of one day finding a cove where they can keep themselves safe from errors and stress. Unfortunately, or perhaps fortunately so, this cove does not exist. Instead managers are given the ability to understand that they are at the service of their situation and the people whom they are responsible for. Thus, being of service becomes the noblest challenge a captain can undertake. And so, the captain instinctively understands that the only way to face the storm is by accepting the waves and violence. His single mission is to go beyond expectations and worry about the men and women who are onboard his ship. This is the strength of this book!

Dominique Steiler

Professor, Director of the Personnel and Managerial Development Centre, Grenoble

Leading Business Change

A Practical Guide to
Transforming Your Organization

Leading Business Change

A Practical Guide to Transforming Your Organization

Karin Stumpf

CRC Press
Taylor & Francis Group
Boca Raton   London   New York

CRC Press is an imprint of the
Taylor & Francis Group, an **informa** business

A PRODUCTIVITY PRESS BOOK

CRC Press
Taylor & Francis Group
6000 Broken Sound Parkway NW, Suite 300
Boca Raton, FL 33487-2742

© 2015 by Karin Stumpf
CRC Press is an imprint of Taylor & Francis Group, an Informa business

No claim to original U.S. Government works

Printed on acid-free paper
Version Date: 20150527

International Standard Book Number-13: 978-1-4987-2657-3 (Hardback)

This book contains information obtained from authentic and highly regarded sources. Reasonable efforts have been made to publish reliable data and information, but the author and publisher cannot assume responsibility for the validity of all materials or the consequences of their use. The authors and publishers have attempted to trace the copyright holders of all material reproduced in this publication and apologize to copyright holders if permission to publish in this form has not been obtained. If any copyright material has not been acknowledged please write and let us know so we may rectify in any future reprint.

Except as permitted under U.S. Copyright Law, no part of this book may be reprinted, reproduced, transmitted, or utilized in any form by any electronic, mechanical, or other means, now known or hereafter invented, including photocopying, microfilming, and recording, or in any information storage or retrieval system, without written permission from the publishers.

For permission to photocopy or use material electronically from this work, please access www.copyright.com (http://www.copyright.com/) or contact the Copyright Clearance Center, Inc. (CCC), 222 Rosewood Drive, Danvers, MA 01923, 978-750-8400. CCC is a not-for-profit organization that provides licenses and registration for a variety of users. For organizations that have been granted a photocopy license by the CCC, a separate system of payment has been arranged.

Trademark Notice: Product or corporate names may be trademarks or registered trademarks, and are used only for identification and explanation without intent to infringe.

Library of Congress Cataloging-in-Publication Data

Stumpf, Karin.
    Leading business change : a practical guide to transforming your organization / Karin Stumpf.
        pages cm
    Includes index.
    ISBN 978-1-4987-2657-3
    1. Organizational change. I. Title.

HD58.8.S7949 2016
658.4'063--dc23   2015002848

Visit the Taylor & Francis Web site at
http://www.taylorandfrancis.com

and the CRC Press Web site at
http://www.crcpress.com

To Hannes

Contents

Foreword: Leading in a World of Constant Change

In our fast-evolving world, change is becoming a constant and the "new normal." Companies are surfing the continuous waves of change more than ever. "Under construction" is more and more part of everyday life in organizations, with multiple change initiatives running in parallel and in complex interaction.

Managers and employees alike are under pressure to deliver and adapt to new and demanding challenges, mostly under restricted time and budget. The increasing amount of initiatives leads to engagement gaps: a wear and tear of words and actions. From a people perspective, the challenge is to activate and ensure engagement—even more in tougher times of change. Bringing in change is hard work and energy intensive. It requires perseverance, dedication, empathy and credibility in intentions and behaviour. To avoid the change spiral leading to chronic strain and to achieve the required pace and performance, all involved parties need to "pull at the same string." Without managing the human part, the desired change is only "halfway down the road," as people make or break success.

It is key that executives and managers take an active part in supporting their company on its transformation journey.

Change leadership is imperative in helping business evolve, with leaders having a key role to play in the change process. In light of the previous discussion, change leadership has become a default responsibility, not an exception to the rule or a one-time exceptional action—and it cannot be delegated. This is an important paradigm shift: moving from managing change (resources) to leading change (people).

As we do not know how the future will look, the key question is: How does an organization need to evolve to be able to deal with uncertainties and ambiguities? Driving change needs to be brought even a decisive step further in enhancing organizational agility and strengthening changeability. On the way forward, this is a key contribution of change leadership in a world of constant change.

Felicitas von Kyaw

HR Director, Organizational Development and Change Management at Vattenfall Continental

Acknowledgment

I would first like to thank all the Mr. and Mrs. Smiths I met as a consultant who inspired me to write this book. Without their questions, their quest, and their constant willingness to challenge their own opinions, I wouldn't have grown to become the professional I am—and I would also have fewer anecdotes to include in this book.

Derek Lewis has had a major role in helping me develop, structure, and write the manuscript. He has been a great help throughout the writing process. Together with Patricia Martinez, he has assisted me in making *Leading Business Change* an easy read for leaders around the world. The graphics were designed by Elinore Ria. Her service makes this book visually stand out.

Most of my gratitude goes to my husband. While I was writing down my thoughts on paper, he regularly questioned my approach and helped me and the book develop. He always is there for me and makes my life richer. Thank you for that, from the bottom of my heart.

Chapter 1

Leading the Journey to Success

> Ich kann freilich nicht sagen, ob es besser werden wird, wenn es anders wird; aber so viel kann ich sagen: es muss anders werden, wenn es gut werden soll.
>
> I cannot say whether things will get better if we change; what I can say is they must change if they are to get better.
>
> **—Georg Christoph Lichtenberg**

Some believe that the success or failure of a new corporate strategy depends on external factors, such as an economic downswing or new industry regulations.

Some believe that success or failure depends on how committed the senior executives are to the project and whether they allocate sufficient resources to see the initiative through.

Others believe the company's culture determines whether a new strategic direction is adopted or abandoned, thinking that the more dynamic the company is, the more open it will be to change.

Still many others see the company's leaders as the core determinant. Some are visionaries who see market trends early on and get there ahead of the competition; the strategic change ultimately succeeds because they saw how to be in the right place at the right time.

There is an element of truth in every one of these perspectives. The global recession derailed many corporate initiatives, for instance. It is a fact that many senior managers do not fully appreciate how complex it is to change companies' processes. Plenty of companies are mired in "the way it's always been done." Visionary Steve Jobs aligned his company with the market before the market even existed.

I know firsthand that all of these elements play a role in the ultimate success or failure of turning corporate strategy into reality. But, every strategic initiative faces these challenges. Every project I know of was affected by the companies' macroenvironments. Nearly every project needs more resources than were originally allocated. Every project faces internal resistance. Companies rarely have prophetic visionaries who can anticipate the market.

As a consultant, first with McKinsey and then Deloitte, I witnessed how projects that should have been successful became sidetracked, merged with other initiatives, were tabled until "a better time," or outright declared a failure. These initiatives represent hundreds of millions of euros in wasted effort and millions more in unrealized potential.

On the other hand, some projects that should never have been approved in the first place succeeded—sometimes against all odds and in the face of fierce opposition. Even absent from the expected factors of success, these initiatives ultimately delivered on their promises to fulfil the original corporate strategies.

After witnessing so many surprising failures and so many surprising successes, I wanted to know what factors determined the outcomes. More important, I wanted to know how they did so. Some of those successes might have been luck, but surely not all of them. There had to be a key factor that, when present, led to success; when absent, to failure.

I studied the problem from both an academic perspective in my postdoctoral research in organizational psychology and from a practical perspective by working with global clients through my own consultancy, Acrasio. After consulting for dozens of companies—from global giants like DaimlerChrysler and Deutsche Bank to midsize organizations like Firmenich and the International Committee of the Red Cross—and studying dozens more, I finally found it.

What Is the Determining Factor in Successfully Turning Strategy into Reality?

After dissecting successful and failed initiatives, after administering surveys to relevant teams and stakeholders, after carefully reviewing my and my colleagues' projects, this is what I found: Failed strategies reflected failed execution.

When I then investigated failed execution, I did not find that it was the result of a poor-performing team, but rather a lack of ownership. Digging still further, I discovered that this lack of ownership came from the project leader's lack of support. That is, success did not hinge on a talented or resourceful leader, but rather a leader who had the broad support of people at different levels throughout the organization: their peers, the people below them, upper management, and others.

Although this may seem like common sense, it is striking to note that the primary cause of failure was not a lack of organizational resources, changing market conditions, or a lack of talent. The major factors of failure were not something beyond the team's—and especially the leader's—control.

To be crystal clear: the success of a change project rests almost entirely in the hands of its leader: You. You, as the leader in charge of implementing a corporate initiative, are the deciding factor. You, Mr. or Ms. Manager, have ultimate responsibility for the success or failure of the collective efforts of the project. Your efforts as the primary agent of change will drive all these other elements.

I do not mean to say that all failures stem from an initiative's leader. As a consultant who works side by side with such corporate managers, I see the obstacles that arise almost daily through no fault of their own. What I have discovered is that all initiatives' leaders have the potential to compensate for all these other challenges.

Although you may not be the cause of the problems you face, you have the capability to overcome them. I like to use the analogy of captaining a ship from one port to another. Every captain has had a different ship and crew than other captains. Some have sailed luxury liners around the world; some paddled canoes from island to island. Some of those luxury liners sank, like the *Titanic*; some of those canoes plied the Polynesian islands for years. Some, like Christopher Columbus, faced fierce opposition from their crews and yet still found a way to arrive at their destinations.

All these captains faced different challenges and conditions. Some factors were completely outside their control. But, the primary determinant of whether the voyage was considered successful or not was because of the captains' actions and reactions in the face of adversity and the unexpected.

You could take this as bad news. After all, "the captain goes down with the ship": If your initiative fails, you will likely be held responsible. If you are formally held responsible, it could result in being denied a promotion or even being fired. If you are informally held responsible, you may have few opportunities for advancement in your company or even in your industry, depending on how well known the failure is.

But, this book is not about how to avoid failure—it is about how to successfully achieve change. I want to show you that despite the negative factors that affect your efforts, you have the ability to skilfully navigate around them to reach your destination.

The Process of Success

I developed my approach from working with in-the-trenches managers and executives who did not have the luxury of time to bridge the gap between a theoretical model and their everyday reality. My model arose from piecing together the best practices of successful leaders (or, at least, successful in a particular aspect of a project). From there, I distilled my observations into a broad framework that can be universally applied, as I have demonstrated from change projects as diverse as those of a Spanish telecommunications provider and a Canadian train manufacturer.

My model does not revolve around an executive team sitting down in a boardroom to have a status meeting, although those meetings are helpful. I designed my approach to be easy to use and remember by a busy manager who has dozens of tasks and responsibilities, only one of which is transforming an aspect of a company to align with the corporate goals. My adaptive methodology is more of a mental framework than a way to characterize typical change steps and to-do lists.

As such, it can be easily remembered as simply "three phases, four questions." When you understand the three phases, you automatically understand where your priorities should be, thereby guiding you to invest your time and effort where they are needed most. The four key questions remain the same in each phase, but their focus changes according to the stage of your project. If you successfully address the four questions in the first phase, they should naturally lead you into the second phase.

But, as they say, the devil is in the details.

The Number-One Challenge

My approach draws from a deceptively simple observation related to the number-one challenge: Change—any kind of business change—is, at its core, about people.

If the effort to expand into a new market was a colossal failure, the truth could be that the respective employees inside the sales and marketing groups failed to appreciate the cultural gaps. If a "company" does not allocate sufficient resources to a project, the reality is that a person or group did not allocate them. If an information technology system cannot be implemented, the real story might be that the test group inside the company was openly hostile to the two system administrators attempting to roll out the system.

Regardless of the scale or scope of your own initiative, the basic idea remains the same. You do not work with the "market," "vendors," "companies," or "systems." Behind all of those generalities lies the common denominator: Ultimately, you work with people.

Shortly after the merger of Daimler-Benz and Chrysler, I was hired to support a technology project. Because both of these corporations were global companies in their own right, they each had offices in almost every country. Because of the nature of the project, I had the opportunity to work with their respective employees around the globe, which let me quickly understand the unique challenges of a merger between these two disparate company cultures.

Although Daimler-Benz was a multinational, it became readily apparent to me that the company was dominated by its German roots. When I called employees in other countries who had been with Daimler-Benz since before the merger, I began speaking in English. I would not expect them to speak either of my native languages (French or German), and they could not expect me to speak theirs. English, I assumed, would be the common denominator. But, the moment they caught even a hint of a German accent, they immediately switched to German. This happened with every nationality I interacted with, from Spain to Vietnam. I later learned that to communicate within the company—that is, to advance— employees were expected to learn the predominant language of Daimler-Benz.

When I conducted workshops with an international cross section of the newly formed company, DaimlerChrysler, I did so in English—again, assuming it was the international language of business. Although the Americans and other nationalities spoke English, of course, we had to hire translators for the German executives. Because they spoke the predominant tongue of their company before the merger, they had never seen the need to learn their counterparts' language.

Consider this for a moment: A company whose organizational language is German (to the degree that its senior-most executives speak almost nothing else) merges with a company whose organizational language is English (to the degree that its senior-most executives speak almost nothing else). What could possibly go wrong?

I was not at all surprised a few years later when Daimler announced it was divesting itself of Chrysler. Not only did Daimler sell Chrysler for $30 billion less than the purchase price, but after covering other losses, Daimler ended up having to pay to get rid of the US carmaker.

A typical change initiative has a much smaller scope than merging two of the world's largest companies. Certainly, there were thousands of details that ultimately contributed to the failure. But, then again, most projects do not have the budget and backing that this one did. Senior management needed this strategic initiative to succeed and was willing to invest as much as they had to—billions, if needed.

I contend that the merger primarily failed not because of the macroeconomic environment, not because of a lack of visionary leadership, not because of insufficient resources— not because of inefficient processes, nor because of anything else along these lines. DaimlerChrysler failed because the respective groups of employees both stayed in their respective figurative places rather than journeying to a new one together. People do not naturally migrate to a new place. They must be led there. Ergo, they need leadership.

The premise of my approach rests on two ideas. The first is that you, the person tasked with implementing the change initiative, have the ability to bring about the change. The second is that your top priority (and problem) is not managing budgets, divisions, companies, or systems, but managing people.

Three Phases, Four Questions

The first phase in my adaptive methodology is to **mobilize**. You must marshal your available resources, that is, the support, time, and energy of key individuals. Once you understand your resources and their buy-in, you can use them as the basis for charting the course of your journey from the present into the ideal future.

The second task is to **crusade**: You must embark on a quest to lead people to a new and better place. For this, you will need to increase your circle of influence—that is, the number of people who actively support you—as you will inevitably encounter hardships and unforeseen circumstances. Everyone does.

Third, you must **populate** the place where you have arrived. That is, you and your team will help the affected employees settle into their new roles and responsibilities and work together to solidify the new changes and new organizational processes.

In each phase, there are four key questions that you must constantly answer (Figure 1.1): Why? Who? What? and Where? Why are we engaging in this phase? Who are the key people in this phase? What are we focussing on in this phase? Where are we headed at the conclusion of this phase?

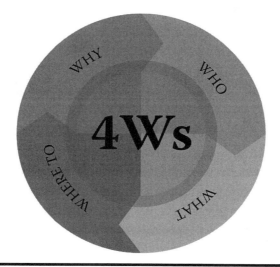

Figure 1.1   The 4Ws: why, who, what and where. To start the mobilization phase, it is crucial to identify the 4Ws. The path to success is realizing what these four components are because they do, after all, define your mission.

Phase I is the mobilization phase:

■ *Why* am I mobilizing?
   To fulfil business needs

■ *Who* am I mobilizing?
   Decision makers

■ *What* am I mobilizing for?
   To identify potential solutions

■ *Where* will mobilizing take me?
   To a decision on a course of action

To summarize the mobilization phase: You must identify unfulfilled business needs with key executives to clarify the common vision and required solutions.

For example, your boss might set a generic goal and ask you to reach it: "We need to achieve 10% market share within three years." There are any number of ways to reach that goal. You could simply buy a competitor and reach the goal instantly, but you could not simply implement that solution without understanding if the initiative has the funding and support personnel to do so. Thus, the mobilization phase begins with clarifying not only what the decision makers want to achieve, but also what resources they are willing to put toward it. At the very end of that potentially lengthy process, you should have a clear idea of the decision makers' own vision (they may simply be thinking of hiring more salespeople) and the parameters of the potential solutions whereby you can achieve it.

Phase II, the crusading phase, is about designing the solution:

- *Why* am I crusading?
  To identify the specific business changes required in the organization

- *Who* am I crusading to?
  Key stakeholders and representatives of all affected stakeholder groups

- *What* am I crusading for?
  To design new organizational structures and processes

- *Where* will crusading take me?
  To effective implementation of the plan

That is, you need to identify the core members of the group and key stakeholder groups who will support you in the design of the organization's new structure and processes leading to the required change.

Everyone wants a hand-picked dream team of talent and experience with which to execute a project. The reality is that you have to work with what you have. In the crusading phase, you are evangelizing a new idea and gaining the support of people outside your core team. This includes internal people, such as your original backers (the decision makers from the mobilization phase), project team members (usually assigned to you by those decision makers), key leaders in directly affected groups (such as someone from the marketing department or a front-line technician), "change agents" (people willing to design and support the new processes and structure), and even other managers (perhaps a peer who had a similar experience or a superior who wants to implement the same solution in his or her division).

The main concept in the crusading phase is that, aside from understanding best practices and deciding on a solution, you are expanding your circle of influence and increasing the number of people who buy in to the need for the change and the new—albeit continually evolving—direction you are leading them.

Phase III is about populating, or the delivery of the needed business changes:

■ *Why* am I populating?
  To ensure individual acceptance of the new processes and structure

■ *Who* am I populating for?
  All affected personnel

■ *What* am I populating for?
  To solidify the new changes

■ *Where* will populating take me?
  To delivery of the original expected results of the initiative

At the end of the initiative, you must ensure that the majority of affected employees are aligned with their new responsibilities and tasks that, collectively, deliver the originally desired results. By the end of the crusading phase, you have defined the solution. The populating phase is also about effectively executing the solution.

Throughout these three phases (Figure 1.2), we will discuss three groups of people who will become part of your eventual "coalition." The first comprises key stakeholders, the people who have a vested interest in the outcome of the solution. The second group is your "team," the group of people actively working with you to design and implement the solution. Third, I'll talk about the impacted employees who have bought in to the vision for change, actively embrace it, and use the new processes.

Nothing Ever Goes According to Plan

This plan looks nice and neat on paper, but the reality of putting this into practice looks quite messy. Corporate strategies change. Vendors go out of business. Key backers suddenly withdraw their support. Employees quit. Nothing ever goes according to plan.

That is why this book is devoted to walking you through how to use this framework to effect change, even in the chaotic reality of every business professional. In addition, I have created a hypothetical scenario centred on Mr. Schmidt, the archetype of the kinds of business managers I work with. His true-to-life experiences begin each chapter as a way of introducing you to the concepts and advice I provide in the body of the chapter. In the chapters dealing with my methodology, you will find a list of questions to challenge your thinking and help you assess where you are in the process.

The bottom line is that change—any kind of change—is a journey in and of itself. Every culture tells the hero's tale, like that of Aladdin or Jonah, wherein the hero undergoes a journey and is transformed by the process. The heroes face

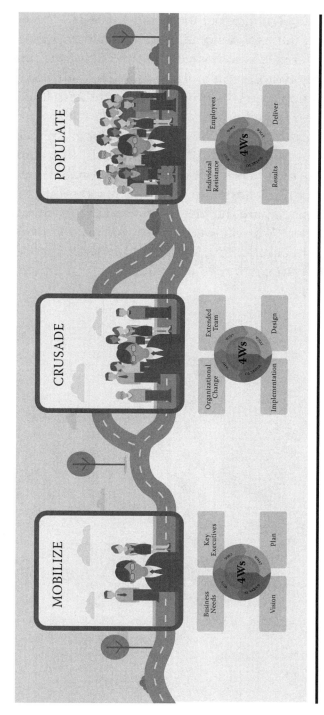

Figure 1.2 The path to success. This graphic serves as a reminder regarding what is important in each phase of your journey, bringing in a key focus to the 4Ws that need to be addressed during that particular phase.

hardship and uncertainty, but ultimately come out the better for having had the experience. Corporate change is much the same. The difference is that instead of one individual undergoing the journey (you), it is a journey of many, many people. But, they still depend on one person to lead them. It all begins—and ends—with you.

Every successful journey has a good leader at the helm. Although there are hundreds, if not thousands, of factors that must work together to bring about organizational change, the vast majority of them are ultimately your responsibility. You, Mr. or Ms. Manager, are the one in whose lap this change project has fallen. You, Mr. or Ms. Manager, are the main determinant of success. You, Mr. or Ms. Manager, have the weight of the company on your shoulders.

Are you ready?

Chapter 2

The Captain for the Journey

Life is change. Growth is optional. Choose wisely.

—William Somerset Maugham

For the first time since he could remember, Mr. Schmidt was sweating before a meeting with his boss.

As the director of accounting, he was used to meeting with the chief financial officer on a regular basis. What made today different was that his boss had given him no clue what the meeting was about. Usually, Mr. Schmidt was ready to answer any questions and make recommendations before ever going in to a meeting. Today, though, he was totally unprepared.

What worried him were the rumours floating around the company about big layoffs. Although the company was financially sound, the market was slowly shrinking, putting pressure on the whole industry. Layoffs were just a matter of time.

He fervently hoped he was not one of them.

"Have a seat, Schmidt," Monsieur Valery said with a cheerful smile. "We have something big to discuss."

Seeing the look of relief on Mr. Schmidt's face, his boss said, "What? Were you worried about something?"

"Frankly, I've been worried about the rumours of layoffs I've been hearing. When you didn't tell me what this meeting was for, I feared the worst."

"No, no, no, Schmidt. This meeting is about those rumours, but we need to talk about something quite the opposite of your fears," Monsieur Valery said.

"Oh?"

"As you know, profits last year weren't as high as we expected. The board has set a goal of 10% cost reduction across all departments. While the other executive heads are preparing for layoffs, hiring freezes and the like, I'm sure it won't be enough. I, on the other hand, plan to deliver on the goal. That's where you come in."

"You're asking me to help you find places where we can save money?" Mr. Schmidt asked.

Monsieur Valery smiled. "No—I'm asking you to head the initiative. I'll have my hands full with a couple of other projects, and you have demonstrated that you are more than capable. This will be your initiative and your responsibility. I'm asking you to deliver on the promise I made to the board of directors."

Mr. Schmidt looked thoughtful for a moment and then said, "I have been working on something you might find interesting. While I haven't nailed down the details, I have been looking into the possibility of outsourcing large portions of the accounts payable functions. I was going to finish my cost-benefit analysis before presenting it to you, but my preliminary results suggest we could save 15% or even 20% of our yearly budget."

"I knew you were the right person for this job,
Schmidt. You've already been doing the work!" He
stood to shake Mr. Schmidt's hand. "Take a few
weeks to thoroughly research it, then we'll present
your idea to the chief executive officer [CEO] and
get his buy-in. I'm looking forward to seeing what
you come up with."

I was once hired by a manufacturing company to provide a
workshop in France to engineering managers on how to coach
their own employees. The central question in the workshop
was, "How can you help your employees become better in
what you expect them to do every day?"

During a break, I had a side conversation with a manager and
asked how my workshop compared to others she had attended.
To my surprise, she said, "This is the first workshop of this type
I've had in over twenty years of being a manager here."

Throughout the day, I discreetly inquired for information
from other participants. One by one, they all confirmed that
this was the first leadership training their employer had ever
provided. Although I was glad the company's owner had
begun investing in the employees (and, moreover, that I had
the opportunity to conduct their first training), I was dismayed
that their managers had gone years—even decades—without
any type of leadership training. The more I conducted these
types of change leadership workshops, seminars, and trainings, the more I learned how common this was.

When I first entered the field of change management, there
was not an established step-by-step process or methodology.
The general consensus in the industry was "communicate and
train." While those are and will always be the key instruments to
effective change management, they are only vague guidelines. If
you want to be an effective change agent, you need more than a
mountain of e-mails and couple of explanatory meetings.

You must be a true leader—not only in explicit authority and responsibility but also in genuine influence. As I will continue to point out throughout this book, the success or failure of a strategic initiative rests largely in your hands. If change begins with you, from where are you starting? Do you have the skills and experience to address your assignment? Or, are you a typical manager, thrust into a leadership role with little or no preparation on how to lead change?

Before you can answer that question, you have to understand what being an effective change leader encompasses. When you undertake a large change initiative, you have a special role, perhaps unlike any one that you have had up to this point. You are no longer a leader forging ahead on the road of "how it has always been done." You have to become a leader modelling "the way we are going to do it from now on."

Being an effective change leader covers five key areas of responsibility:

1. Modelling the role
2. Motivating people
3. Mediating resistance
4. Shaping the change
5. Communicating the change

Your success, and the ultimate success of the initiative, will directly depend on how successful you are in each of these five areas. Although the concept of leadership is bigger than any one book—much less one chapter—allow me to briefly address these five key leadership concepts as they relate to change management.

Modelling the Role

Changing organizational processes and structures really comes down to changing individuals' behaviour. As such, it is critical that you model the behaviour you expect to see from affected stakeholder groups.

For example, an accounts payable process is usually rigid, with any number of checks and balances. If you do not model the behaviour of adhering to the established protocols, should it come as a surprise that others in the company follow your lead?

Does your conduct reflect the conduct you expect from the affected personnel? If you "talk the talk" but do not "walk the walk," then you can expect your employees to do the same. Although they may pay lip service to the new expectations, like you, they will continue to do things the way they want to.

Being a role model goes beyond just leading in the way you act. Who was it that said, "If you're leading but no one's following, you're just taking a walk." An effective role model is out in front, but behind them is a group of followers.

The question, then, is how do you get people to follow you? During trainings like the one I mentioned previously, I ask participants, "What do you feel is the key element in a person being a role model?" The majority of my change management trainees say, in one way or another, "Showing respect." When I ask them to explain, they follow up their answer with, "Showing respect for others' opinions and perspectives."

I cannot underscore this critical concept enough. Let me slightly rephrase what they said: "If you want us to follow your leadership, first show us that you care about what we think." This is the real-world embodiment of that old saying, "People don't care how much you know until they know how much you care." Before you can expect someone to follow your actions as a role model for change, you must first pay attention to their ideas.

Motivating Other People

Listening to others may seem like an elementary idea, but I am continually surprised by how few managers attempt it. As the person in charge of a strategic initiative, you presumably have some degree of explicit authority. You can order people to accomplish certain tasks and tell them to comply with certain policies. But, as long as you have to force them to take action, you may have their obedience, but you will never have their buy-in. The more effective approach is to motivate your stakeholders.

When I presented this idea as a central tenet in change leadership, a client of mine noted how difficult it is for leaders "to always be so full of energy and so positive." She pointed to how much of an effort it is to maintain that level of enthusiasm. By the time you are through, you need your own motivator. Although she embraced the spirit of motivation, she missed the main point. Motivating other people goes beyond being peppy and enthusiastic. It is about finding the obstacles that keep individuals from providing their full support and understanding their concerns.

Take the Sprint–Nextel fiasco, for example. Its employees sued the company for millions in unpaid sales commissions. The company admitted that it had never been able to properly integrate the multiple back-end information technology systems across its merged operations. (This is yet another example of a major change project gone awry.) If you were put in charge of integrating these systems, it would not matter how bubbly and happy you were. Much of your team would remain unmotivated because their basic concern—getting paid their rightful commissions—would remain unresolved.

However, you might be able to turn this situation around by that very fact. If you demonstrated how working together to integrate those systems would result in everyone being paid, you could very well have an incredibly motivated team. In that case, you would not have to be peppy at all, but it would not affect the esprit de corps.

Motivation is mostly intrinsic. That means people find their motivation inside themselves, rather than drawing from the environment around them. As a change leader, your task is to create an environment in which they can thrive, where they find fulfilment, and where they know that they make a difference. You know you have accomplished this goal when your team can honestly say, "My job is meaningful. I can positively influence the outcome of my efforts. Moreover, my manager inspires me to deliver great work." Shared ownership of the change is one of the keystones of my methodology.

In the end, you want people working *with* you to execute change—not working *for* you to fulfil a set of tasks.

Mediating Resistance

When you empower people to participate in the process of change instead of resisting it, you are inviting them to share their view on how to best achieve it. Of course, many people's viewpoints will differ from yours and from each other's—some even in vehement opposition to one another.

As the person in charge, you can make unilateral decisions (and, in many cases, you must). But, if you continually run roughshod over others, you will undermine their motivation and receive their begrudging efforts—not their best ideas and sincere interest.

As a mediator, you need to get everyone's ideas on the table, facilitate a discussion, arrive at a unified approach for how to tackle the issues at hand, and then work on positively addressing the dissenting opinions. The best way to mediate opposing viewpoints is to be prepared in the first place. In your first encounter with a stakeholder, gather basic information, gauge their support, and take the opportunity to listen to their concerns and ideas. Before arriving at the outcome of everyone's input, you can discuss the pros and cons of individual stakeholders' suggestions. That way, people can see that you at least seriously and sincerely considered what they said, even if their ideas ultimately were not integrated into the solution.

Also, view opposition for what it is: apprehension to change. People in general fear change because change automatically means "challenge" and "the unknown." We would much rather deal with what we expect than face the unexpected.

Be proactive. Instead of waiting for opposition, go find it. Talk to the heads of departments to involve them early on. Talk to people who will be directly affected, not only to inform them of the proposed changes, but also to gather information on what their concerns are. The more you address people's fears, and the earlier you do so, the smoother your project will go.

In spite of your best efforts, though, you may still encounter entrenched resistance. If you have the authority, you may simply exercise it if you are left with no other options. But, often the resistance you face may be beyond your control. I once had a project where a key executive pushed back when it came time to implement the company's solution. As the consultant, I could not simply order him to comply. After exhausting other methods of mediating his viewpoint, as a last resort I asked the CEO to step in. The CEO's solution was to add the outcome of the change project as one of the executive's key performance indicators (KPIs). From that moment, I never had an issue receiving the executive's full support and cooperation. Although not the method of mediation I would have hoped for, by doing so I mitigated his opposition so that the project could move forward.

Shaping the Change

Most leaders understand their role as a change shaper. As we explored in the previous section, at times you may have to make the hard decisions and move forward with the project. As the change leader, you are ultimately responsible not only for the eventual delivery of the expected results, but also the intermediate shape of the solution as you and your team create it. Although you should motivate your team members and solicit their input, you must balance that with being able to make the call at the appropriate time.

That necessarily entails being able to take a risk, being willing to admit mistakes, and seeing how your decisions will affect the rest of the organization. By definition, your initiative will force the company to change. As the shaper of change, you must guide your organization—that is, the stakeholders' groups inside and outside your company—to evolve and adapt to the new vision.

At times, your journey will feel like it takes two steps forward and one step back, but you cannot allow setbacks to demoralize you. Unless and until your superiors relieve you of your responsibility, you must continue to shape the efforts of your team, regardless of the circumstances.

I have seen too many managers fear mistakes. They want to spend so much time trying to make sure they "get it right the first time" that their inaction leads to the entire project's immobilization. In business as in life, you cannot move forward by standing still.

Take ownership, as it is not only your explicit authority to make decisions but also your responsibility to do so.

Communicating the Change

Here is an odd question for you: What is the most frequented resource on a typical company's intranet? I will even help you by telling what it is not: It is not the list of policies and procedures, the human resources page, or the company news. Of the vast pool of resources available to the workforce of an average corporation, the most accessed page is—the canteen page.

That is right: The most overwhelmingly important thing to an employee is what is on the cafeteria's lunch menu. The information they seek most is, not coincidentally, what is most relevant to them. Keep this insightful fact in mind when you assume your fifth and final key responsibility as a change leader: communicating the change.

Communicating can involve any method of doing so. We live in a fortunate age where we have a multitude of channels to use, from e-mail to video chat to social media. At the same time, because we are bombarded by so much information, much of it simply becomes white noise.

The proliferation of communication channels has not closed the gap of miscommunication. How many times have you spoken to someone who "didn't get your e-mail," only to look back through their inbox and find it sitting there, unread? How many times have you been guilty of this yourself?

When you communicate your issues, you cannot assume that your message got through. Even if the other person read the memo or heard your talk, they may not have understood what you needed to convey.

Just as with the other four areas of responsibility, you must be proactive in your communication. If you send out a global e-mail, follow up with key recipients to ensure they took away the key message. If you have a team meeting, make sure that you later find the people who did not speak up to see why they did not participate. In short, take responsibility not only for broadcasting your message but also for making sure it was clearly received.

Communication experts tell us that 90% of communication is non-verbal. Much of it is body language, such as a facial expression or a guarded pose. Therefore, the most effective communication method is face to face. By engaging in a one-on-one phone call, you may be able to hear the reluctance in someone's immediate response to your words; in a meeting, you can see their face and watch their posture. By gathering these non-verbal cues, you can gauge how much support you have from that person. In addition, in a one-on-one setting, they may be more open to bringing up potential problems sooner, rather than letting you encounter them later.

But, here is where we return to the intranet-canteen fact: When communicating with anyone, what they want to hear is how your message is relevant to their everyday life. Although plenty of employees truly want to see their company, division, group, or team succeed, their own personal success is naturally more important to them. When you begin talking about doing things differently, changing "the way it's always been done," or "improving the process," people often hear: "Here's more work; we're going to try something new and untested and maybe you'll be fired."

I picture Maslow's hierarchy of needs. At the base of the pyramid is food and water. The next level up is safety and security, such as keeping their job so they can pay the rent or mortgage. After that, they look to love and belonging, which might take the form of their family's respect or remaining in their established community of peers. All of this culminates in one fact: Your strategic initiative is a distant priority to them.

When you communicate, do not just communicate what you want the person to know. Communicate what the person needs to hear as well as what the person wants to hear. Tell the person how the initiative will benefit or affect them. Make it emotionally appealing. Use pictures and analogies to make it more impactful.

Effective communication means getting your message across in a way that is effective for your immediate audience.

Embracing Your Role as a Change Leader

While working for McKinsey, I was assigned to work in the Vienna office of my employer. (As you may well imagine, it was beautiful.) There were four of us assigned to the project— three men and myself. One day, one of my colleagues was trying to open a water bottle. After a few frustrating attempts, one of the other consultants attempted to open it. Then, the third consultant tried to open it. All were unsuccessful. Finally, I said, "Here, let me try."

They laughed at me. How could I, a woman, hope to open a bottle that three men in their prime could not? Smiling, they stood around me to witness this feat of strength. Silently, I untied my silk scarf, wrapped it around the bottle cap, twisted it free, and handed it back to the first consultant. After a moment of surprise, he said, "Well, I could have done that." I thought to myself, *but you didn't.*

This is the same attitude I have with my clients when I present these five traits of leadership. They are common-sense traits—but they are not commonplace. All executives could cultivate these seemingly straightforward traits—but they do not.

You cannot achieve lasting change without being an effective change leader, and you cannot be an effective change leader without being effective in each of these five key areas. It does take more upfront effort to motivate your team members than it would to simply order them to do something. Creating relationships with and between people requires an investment of time. Mastering these traits is not easy.

But, would you not rather make the effort and create a self-sustaining momentum, with support at all levels and from all stakeholder groups, than continually fight against the current and deal with opponent after opponent? Would it not be easier to create a coalition of people working in tandem toward the same goal than to be the Lone Ranger trying to herd everyone in the same direction?

I promise you: It is far easier when everyone is behind you and pulling in the same direction than for you to be behind them, pushing them in the same direction.

PHASE I

MOBILIZE

Envisioning the Solution

At the beginning of your project, you probably have some goals identified by upper management that have defined parameters and potential support resources. After evaluating your own capabilities in leading this effort, your first step is to clearly understand what the real goals are, what resources you have, what the current reality is, and what potential ways you can use all those elements to deliver the hoped-for results.

The overarching questions you must answer throughout the mobilization phase are the following:

■ *Why* am I mobilizing?
   To fulfil business needs

■ *Who* am I mobilizing?
   Decision makers

■ *What* am I mobilizing for?
   To identify potential solutions

■ *Where* will mobilizing take me?
   To decide on a course of action

Chapter 3

Determining the Destination

Nul vent n'est bon pour celui qui n'a pas de port de destination.

No wind serves him who has no port of destination.

—Michel de Montaigne

Mr. Schmidt touched down in Paris just before sunset. After checking into his hotel, he ate a quick bite in the restaurant downstairs and turned in early.

The next morning, he met Monsieur Valery for breakfast.

"So, are you ready to present this to senior management?" his boss asked.

Mr. Schmidt said, "This will be my first presentation to the CEO [chief executive officer], but I feel confident. I think I've put together a compelling case."

"Excellent, excellent. You know we're the only department to offer something as ambitious as this. All the other chief execs are talking about trimming corners or laying off a few people here and there. Finance is the only department to come up with something bold," Monsieur Valery said.

"Do you think the CEO will go for it?"

"To be honest, Schmidt, the CEO has already assured me that he'll approve the project. Today's meeting is to get the other execs on board and demonstrate how you're going to go about the project."

By midmorning, Mr. Schmidt was standing in the boardroom outlining the outsourcing plan to the CEO, CFO [chief financial officer], COO [chief operating officer], CMO [chief marketing officer], and CIO [chief information officer].

At the presentation's conclusion, the CIO spoke up: "Mr. Schmidt, you have obviously put a lot of effort into the possibility of outsourcing accounts payable, but are you aware we tried outsourcing the information technology [IT] technical support functions about two years ago?"

Mr. Schmidt tried to hide his surprise. "No, I'm afraid I was unaware of that fact."

The CIO said, "Well, we did, and it didn't go very well. The company we outsourced to turned out to be incompetent. In fact, after only two months into the outsourcing, we were scrambling to undo the whole project. I hope you have better luck."

Mr. Schmidt let the matter drop, but for the first time, he recognized the doubt in the other executives' eyes. To his relief, the CEO wasn't one of them.

At the end of the meeting, the CEO said, "Thank you. As I said earlier, your boss believes the cost savings of this project will be substantial and has thrown his full support behind it. As such, we are allocating a budget for you to work with, so please move forward and keep us updated on your progress."

When Mr. Schmidt arrived home that evening, his wife could immediately tell something was wrong.

After she asked, he said, "I feel like I've been blindsided. I thought all the senior execs were supporting this project. As it is, it's just Valery and the CEO. The CIO openly voiced his doubts."

His wife suggested, "Why not try to win them to your side? Why not approach the CIO and get his input on why it didn't work out?"

He paused for a minute. "You know, you're right. If I could get the CIO involved, I just might get him to take some ownership of the project." He snapped his fingers. "That's what I'll do. I'll get Valery to set up a conference call between the three of us to get us on the same page."

He picked up the phone to call his boss.

While a consultant at Deloitte, I interviewed a client about a customer relationship management (CRM) solution he wanted to implement throughout the entire company. If you have ever been part of a company-wide software rollout, you know how much of a challenge it is. It requires process design, data migration, training, role transitioning, system customization and more, representing potentially millions of euros in labour hours and direct costs, plus the opportunity costs. It is a substantial investment, to say the least.

In preparation for the project, I asked the executive a simple question: "Why do you want to implement a CRM solution?"

He said, "Well, our major competitor did, so we should probably do it, I guess."

I could barely believe what I had heard. This project would involve thousands of employees and countless lost hours of productivity. It would be a major disruption in their everyday business operations. Yet, senior management made the decision based on the fact that because "everybody else" was doing it, they should also do it.

Unfortunately, this is typical. Businesses often initiate a new project or plan with no clear connection between it and the company's strategic goals. In fact, senior management sometimes goes ahead with a major project without good alignment between it and even their own expectations.

In one of my first consulting projects through Acrasio, there were two key executives overseeing a major change project. I scheduled meetings with one executive and had him summarize his goals. After a lengthy discussion, he concluded by saying, "The changes will be quite comprehensive."

In my meeting with the other executive, she waved her hand dismissively, saying, "I don't expect this will impact many people."

Immediately, the alarms began going off in my head. Here were the two sponsors for this project with two completely different perspectives on what they were about to undertake. I knew the gap between them had to be addressed before anything else could move forward. I scheduled a meeting between the three of us. Neither of them wanted to attend. After negotiating between them, I finally succeeded in getting them to agree to a ten-minute conference call.

I began the meeting by asking some simple questions. Within just a few minutes, they saw the enormity of the problem. They both had completely different expectations about the size and scope of the project. What was supposed to be a short meeting stretched into two and a half hours as we discussed and solidified the parameters of the project.

That "ten-minute meeting" easily saved ten weeks' worth of effort.

Who Are the Decision Makers?

You might think that the previous story was about clarifying the vision of the change project. From one angle, it was. However, it also pointed to the important idea that you must clearly identify the decision makers. Who are the real sponsors behind the initiative?

When you are given an assignment or volunteer for a project, its seeds were likely sown long before you became part of it. Your first task as a change leader is to identify the key decision makers who can start or stop your new initiative with just a word. Some may already support you, but some may outright oppose you. The corporate sponsors who support you are the beginning of your coalition. Eventually, your circle of influence (see Figure 3.1) will expand to encompass all

Figure 3.1 Your circle of influence. At the beginning of your journey, you might feel alone and without supporters, but as a change leader, it is in your best interest to influence those around you, especially key players, which will make your change journey all the more successful.

affected stakeholder groups, but in the beginning, your focus is on these key executives who control the budget and key resources you need.

You have to ensure there is complete alignment between their goals and the direction in which you are working. It is hoped that their goals align with the organization's stated strategy, but you may have to execute someone's goals that may be misaligned with your company's corporate strategy. However, for long-term success, it is absolutely necessary to align all three at the beginning of your initiative: corporate strategy, executive sponsor's aims and your efforts.

Clarifying the Strategic Objective

Once you have identified your initiative's sponsors, you need to clarify their actual strategic objective and keep this separate from the plan you eventually execute to achieve it. In Mr. Schmidt's case, the stated objective is to reduce costs company-wide. But he and his boss bypassed discussing the many ways this could be achieved, instead going straight to the conclusion that the accounts payable department could be outsourced.

They could achieve the overall goal any number of ways. They could streamline processes. They could upgrade their IT infrastructure. They could train employees in time management. They could consolidate worldwide operations into one central location. But, instead of developing multiple potential solutions and analyzing the pros and cons of each, they selected the one that seemed the most appealing.

Plus, outsourcing a department to another country sounds more impressive than "streamlining internal operations." In the real world, executives and corporate sponsors sometimes undertake projects that are more beneficial to themselves than they are for the company. Far too many big-name mergers and expansion plans have more to do with a person's ego and bragging rights than practicality.

That is not to say that you cannot have both. Plenty of successful change initiatives have achieved the desired results and enhanced the reputations of the core backers. To be an effective change leader, you must recognize that there are two sets of goals (the company's and the sponsor's) that, although they are hoped to be complementary, may not perfectly overlap.

Identifying Stakeholder Groups

After you have clearly identified the sponsor's desired outcome, you need to identify the stakeholder groups affected by your efforts. Because they will bear the brunt of the change, they usually feel that they have the most to lose. As such, they have a keen interest in your project's development.

Mr. Schmidt has clearly failed to identify the various stakeholder groups in his project. Stakeholders are not just the people immediately affected by the initiative. They are anyone, anywhere, who has a stake in the outcome of the project. For instance, the CIO has a personal interest: If the outsourcing project turns out to be a success, it may reflect badly on his own department's outsourcing failure. As a chief executive, the CIO can exert a powerful influence to erode the project's support.

Once Mr. Schmidt identifies this, he should work toward winning this key stakeholder's support. He could sell the CIO on the idea that, should he throw his support behind the new outsourcing project, he could reap the benefits of it being successful. In other words, Mr. Schmidt needs to be ready to let his success also become the CIO's success.

So, Mr. Schmidt overlooked an important stakeholder in upper management. But, perhaps equally important, he has overlooked the stakeholder groups underneath or beside him: every individual who will be affected by the project. Because the change initiative involves accounting, potentially the entire company will be affected in some form or another. Just as Mr. Schmidt had to make the case for the project to senior management, he should also present the project to the other groups who will be affected by the project to whatever degree. This would include at least the procurement team, the legal department, all financial-related positions and human resources. Moreover, he needs to translate the overall benefits of the project into the specific, compelling benefits for each group, cascading down to all employees. What might be interesting for a director might be meaningless for a front-line employee. In your own initiative, you cannot underestimate the need for people from all levels to be respected and involved in some way or another.

In the mobilization phase, your goal is not to solicit direct input from every potentially affected person. Rather, you must identify key stakeholders who either wield considerable influence or can serve as a representative of large groups of stakeholders. When my company is hired to help implement change initiatives, one particularly effective tool is a stakeholder round table. I might bring in representatives from purchasing, IT, managers at all levels, and accounting and then lay out the primary objectives and activities the project would involve. I go around the room, asking each person: "How would these changes reflect in your day-to-day activities? How would they affect your department?" This way, my client and I can gauge to what degree different teams will be impacted by the planned initiative.

Although the first level of alignment is placing the initiative within the context of the company's strategic goals, the second is to place the initiative within the context of each stakeholder group's goals. That, of course, begins with an understanding of who your stakeholder groups are. There are many within the company, but there also are those outside the company. One of the most critical—and yet, for some reason, most often overlooked—is your customers.

Commerzbank, for example, did a wonderful job of keeping its customers involved in a major merger with another global player, Dresdner Bank. They invited a representative sample of their customers—called the Kundenbeirat—into the initiative to represent their different customer groups. Their input was invaluable as the company planned its change.

Besides your customers, you need to identify other external stakeholder groups. For example, in most European countries nearly any type of major change initiative is subject to approval by the local works council. The council can veto an entire project. In many other industrialized countries, you may need to consider workers' unions that exert a powerful influence. Involving representatives from such groups early on helps to make sure that your efforts are not later derailed.

Your foremost objective at the beginning of any change project should be to bring representatives of your stakeholder groups together to ensure there is a common understanding of the need for strategic change and how your plan of action addresses that need. But, to be truly effective, that communication cannot be one way. You must continually receive regular updates, participate in meetings, be in communication on an ongoing basis, and continually receive feedback from the respective groups to enable two-way communication.

Alignment is not a one-time activity. It is an ongoing process that begins from the moment an idea is born and continues until well after it has been implemented.

Challenge Questions

1. Are the objectives that you want to achieve with the business change clear?
2. Do you know who the people who will have a say in the implementation of the business change are?
3. Do the different key stakeholders agree on the planned objectives of the initiative?
4. Will the key stakeholders take an active role in facilitating the business change?
5. How do you plan to regularly update the key stakeholders and keep them and your approach in alignment?

Chapter 4

Taking Stock
of Ship and Crew

Malum quidem nullum esse sine aliquo bono.

There is, to be sure, no evil without something good.

—Latin proverb

Mr. Schmidt stood at the front of a meeting room
with the half-dozen people who comprised his core
project team. After introductions, he quickly out-
lined the outsourcing plan.

"As you can see, we're still in the planning
phase. We're going to have to work closely together
to ensure everything goes smoothly. Before we
begin brainstorming all the tasks and activities
involved, does anyone have any questions?"

A senior accountant spoke up: "Let me make
sure I understand this. We're going to work on an
accounting outsourcing project that, if successful,
will put me on an early retirement plan? You're
asking me to work myself out of a job? And, what

about the other five people sitting here? What about the accounts payable people in our branch offices? What are you planning to do with their jobs? If their positions are outsourced, then they lose their jobs?"

Mr. Schmidt said, "I'm sure—I mean, I know HR [human resources] has a retraining program; I'm sure they'll help everyone find a position somewhere."

The accountant's face clearly showed what he thought of that answer.

Two weeks later, the CFO [chief financial officer] called him in for a status report. "How is the project going?"

"Well, as you know, we're in the information gathering part of the project right now. I . . . I had no idea how bad it was. I've spent the past two weeks speaking with accounting personnel from all of our global offices. Every country, without exception, goes according to its own processes. They spend an enormous amount of time later converting everything into the format we require for quarterly reporting. But, in the meantime, nobody tries to work in a more standardized way."

Monsieur Valery nodded. "I was afraid of that. But the good thing is that that's what this project should address. Think of the efficiency of having all of those tasks performed all by the same team. Speaking of teams, how is our accounting team coming together? Do you need anything?"

Mr. Schmidt hesitated. Just an hour ago, he had gotten off the phone with the regional CFO in Brazil, who flatly told him that she did not need or want corporate headquarters "digging through my books." He had encountered similar resistance everywhere else. His own internal team also showed reticence, complaining that they did not

have time to do their day-to-day jobs on top of a
major outsourcing project. In truth, he had confided
to his wife that, despite the backing of the senior
execs and a decent budget, he was not sure he had
all the resources he truly needed.

But, in front of his boss, he smiled bravely.
"Mmm, there are a few people who are upset about
the coming changes. You know how it is—there are
some in every group. Nothing to really worry about."

The CFO said, "Great! That's good to hear. Keep
me informed. We'll be celebrating success before
we know it."

It would be wonderful if we could choose the people we
work with. It would be ideal if we had our pick of talent. It
would be incredible if they also had great personalities and
enthusiasm for the project. But, as the English proverb says,
"If wishes were horses, beggars would ride." Wishful thinking rarely gets us anywhere. Instead, we almost always have
to work with what we have. Most executive leaders have
resources (time, people and money) assigned to them rather
than being able to choose them on their own.

Remember my previous example of a key manager with-
holding his support until I went to the chief executive officer
(CEO). His solution was to make the project one of the manager's key performance indicators (KPIs), and then I quickly
had his full cooperation. I could not have circumvented the
manager's opposition without the support of his boss. But,
because the CEO had bought into the project, he was willing
to exercise his authority. Without that support, I would have
had few alternatives to mitigate the opposition. The manager
would have continued to withhold his support and that aspect
of the merger might have been a failure instead of the success
it was. (Keep in mind that I earned that support by aligning
my goals with the CEO's goals, which were, in turn, aligned

with the company's stated strategic objectives. This is the critical takeaway from Chapter 3.)

The mobilization phase is about assessing the current situation so that you understand where you are starting from and—just as important—what you are starting with. As a change leader, when we think of the resources we have at our disposal, we generally think of personnel (the people assigned to support us on the project, to whatever degree) and budget. Both of those are important, but before we discuss them, we need to talk about a resource far more important that you may not even realize you have.

Assembling Your Coalition

It is not people. It is not money. It is not even time. It is other people's support. Obviously, I did not have the CEO "at my disposal" to use as an explicit resource to manage the challenging executive. Yet, in a way, I did. Because the CEO was invested in the successful outcome of the project, he used his own considerable resources to help me.

When taking stock of the resources you have, think about the support of your initiative's sponsors and the key stakeholders who have been receptive to it. Whatever amount of explicit resources you have in the form of personnel and budget is small compared to the implicit resources you may have via your supporters.

The concept of influence and the act of expanding your circle of influence are critical to your success. With each additional supporter, your total available resources are multiplied many times what you were originally allocated by your superiors.

But, do not be discouraged if, in the mobilization phase, you do not have a long list of supporters. When the outcome of your project is uncertain, many people will withhold their support and additional resources because they do not want to be identified with something that might not have a positive outcome.

An old proverb says that success has a hundred fathers, but failure is an orphan—people like to be associated with a success, but nobody likes to be associated with a failure. Therefore, at the beginning of a project (just like a new market or product), most people have a tendency to wait. They want to see which way the wind is blowing. If they do support you, it is usually cautious support.

Ironically, the more success you have, the more resources will be made available to you. When your colleagues or superiors see that you are on track to succeed, they are more willing to invest in your project. The more wins you have (that they are aware of), the more that people inside and outside your team will actively and positively support the initiative.

With one client of mine, we put in place a knowledge management and collaboration tool. I regularly requested to have more resources brought on board, but every time the managing director would decline. Our team encountered a lot of resistance in the worldwide deployment until the last four months of the project. By that point, everyone in the company could see that the initiative would inevitably succeed. Then, our much-needed (and often-requested) resources were suddenly made available and brought on board. From then on, we enjoyed all the support we could possibly want.

On the other hand, if the outcome will negatively affect them—as in the case of potential layoffs with Mr. Schmidt's team—they will withdraw their support and may even actively undermine your efforts. The corporate benefits of your project will not always translate into individual benefits.

How can you tell that you have someone's support? It is not enough for someone to tell you, "Oh, yes, I agree. I fully support your outsourcing initiative." Positive and public verbal support is a must-have, but actions speak louder than words. Your backers must support you in deed as well.

In Mr. Schmidt's case, this would be like the CIO telling him, "I support your project, and I'd like to help it be a success. How about if I ask the leader of our initiative to have a meeting with you to discuss her experience?" That is, the CIO would go beyond verbal support and direct one of his employees to give her time and insights. He would take specific action to contribute to Mr. Schmidt's success.

Another example might be the CEO saying, "I understand there will be some upfront costs in getting this project under way, so we are allocating an additional $100,000 from our discretionary funds for this initiative." The CEO would not be just paying lip service to the effort but would be "putting his money where his mouth is," as the Americans say.

Inventorying Available Skill Sets

You want to aim for the support of others, especially key stakeholders who can disproportionately influence the outcome of your project. But, you also need to assess your team—the personnel you have been explicitly assigned to assist you in the design and implementation of the eventual solution.

If your team is like most, the people in it were chosen based on their availability—and, it is hoped, their willingness and knowledge. They may have just finished with another project, they may have been transferred from a division that will be shut down, or their boss may simply perceive that they have extra time on their hands.

Ideally, the people who compose your team should be chosen based on their skills. The expertise they lend to the project will be the primary determinant of success (especially in the early stages) versus how much time they have per day to devote to the project. As the change leader, you want to focus on the quality of their contribution—not the quantity.

I have seen too many executives assume that someone who is used to working a process—whether that be a manufacturing line, as in a factory worker, or a routine process line, as in HR approvals—should have no issue contributing to a project. This is a serious mistake. You cannot assume that a productive employee in a rote process will be just as motivated and productive in a project. These are two completely different working environments.

Outside the projects, performance is usually scripted and outcomes are measurable. Even in the daily and varied challenges that, for instance, information technology (IT) personnel continually face, there is an expected scope of work functions and responsibilities. Regardless of how chaotic or high pressure a position may be, once someone becomes used to it, they establish something of a routine.

Large initiatives, in contrast, have speed, logic and dynamic unique to them. They are different and apart from the team participants' norm. As such, people unused to the fast pace, increased uncertainty and constantly evolving expectations might be completely overwhelmed.

Then, these participants' respective supervisors also may not be used to having their employees pulled aside for a new initiative. Line managers, for instance, are often unwilling to allow their personnel any degree of flexibility to work on a new project. They expect their direct reports to continue doing their regular job just as they always have, leaving it up to them to find some way to put additional time toward their new project tasks.

Although such supervisors may not be directly involved in your project, their support (or lack thereof) directly affects your team's performance. When assessing your team members' contributions, make sure you take into account these external stakeholders. You may even go so far as to intercede on your team members' behalf, selling the benefits of the project and especially their direct reports' involvement.

Keep in mind that your circle of influence may include people completely outside your initiative.

Assessing the Current Situation

Every voyage has a beginning and an ending, but you cannot chart the course unless you know where both points are.

You have been tasked with changing a situation or tackling an issue, but what does it look like right now? How can you know which way to go unless you first know where you are? The mobilization phase entails assessing the support you have in order to make a change, but you must also assess the reality of the current situation.

One of my more high-profile projects was the merger between two large service companies. When I was hired, the decision to merge the two had already been made and the resources available for the project already allocated. My specific task was to support the merger of the two institutional cultures. Of course, before I could propose a plan to do so, I needed to understand what the present looked like.

Both companies were founded and headquartered in Germany and in the same industry. On the outside looking in, you might not think that there would be much of a challenge in merging the two cultures. It would be tempting to skip the assessment altogether.

But, even though both companies comprised German employees, the two companies had two very different perspectives. One's core business was retail, and it also served small- and medium-size enterprises. This company was more "German"—that is, conservative, pragmatic, methodical and more focussed on the domestic market. The other company, by comparison, had a strong international division. Although ostensibly a German institution, much of its workforce was actually British. This company was more open to risk, more focused on larger investments and more globally oriented.

At the outset, this might sound similar to the DaimlerChrysler experience I related previously. The difference between these two mergers is that these service companies recognized the vast cultural differences between the two of them and proactively addressed them. With such open and continuing support for the specific initiative of establishing a unified culture, we eventually arrived at a successful solution.

But, it began with being forthright about their two different starting points.

Likewise, in the mobilizing phase of your initiative, I cannot emphasize enough how important doing a complete assessment is. Without understanding where you are, what the reality is, and what resources you have for your journey, you cannot fully prepare to arrive at your destination.

Challenge Questions

1. What skills and resources are required to actively work on your initiative?
2. To what degree does your team fulfil these requirements?
3. How have you planned to overcome the gaps?
4. What groups will be affected by your initiative, both inside and outside your organization?
5. Do you fully understand how resistant they may be to the planned changes and why?

Chapter 5

Setting the Course

Caminante, no hay camino,
Se hace camino al andar.

Traveler, there is no path;
The path is made by walking.

—Antonio Machado

"Good morning, Schmidt. Coffee?" Monsieur Valery
asked, already motioning the server over.

"Yes, please," Mr. Schmidt replied, sitting down
at the table.

"You look quite pleased with yourself. I trust the
project is going well?"

Mr. Schmidt smiled. "Yes, I'm quite happy. As
of yesterday, everything is on track. The consulting company I hired to manage the outsourcing has
impressed me. On the first day, they had a clear
project plan charting out exactly how things will
progress over the next six months. In their experience, the budget I've given them to work with covers
everything. I've thoroughly reviewed the proposed
milestones and action plan. They are going to take

care of much of the detail work, which frees up my team to focus on the processes we need to change."

The CFO [chief financial officer] nodded while he finished chewing his breakfast. "That's great news. The CEO [chief executive officer] was glad to hear you have hired some support. And they came highly recommended?"

"Yes. This consultancy has successfully managed a few outsourcing projects. It's something of a specialty of theirs. We went over all the best practices they have learned from their experiences and others'. They have an impressive knowledge base," Mr. Schmidt said.

"That's very good to hear, Schmidt. Now, tell me about how you're planning for the change management aspects of the project."

Mr. Schmidt frowned for a split second before regaining his composure. "Well, we have planned for key components, and we will send out e-mails to accounting and finance employees once we have everything in place and begin the transition. We will keep everyone directly affected by the changes continuously updated. I'm confident in the consultants' plan to stay on top of the change management."

Monsieur Valery shook his head. "I'm not sure about that. I have heard from employees and supervisors throughout the department who are upset. From what I've gathered from you and them, we have too many different processes. It's going to be quite a challenge to transition to one streamlined process outsourced to another company. Do you really think this project can move everyone from doing it their own way to the best way—in less than six months?"

"I know it seems like a lot," Mr. Schmidt replied, "but this isn't a problem. We're going to take the proposal from the consultants, based on best practices from the field, and get buy-in from all the financial heads. They know their current practices are not standardized and can stand improvement. They're just resistant to change, that's all. They'll sign off after they see how much easier it's going to make their lives."

As he signed the restaurant bill, Monsieur Valery said, "All right. Keep me apprised of your progress. We're all anxious to make sure this succeeds. We're in seventeen countries and expanding as we speak. We can't have the finance department slip up."

In a manufacturing client's inventory management project we once did, the managing director indicated all the people the company planned to layoff once the project was over. Most of them knew it. Unsurprisingly, they showed little interest in the project's successful outcome. They were completely unmotivated (which returns to our discussion about your challenges in change leadership). Because my consultancy was responsible for the outcome of the project, imagine our predicament.

Once we identified this glaring issue, I presented the difficulty to the client in an effort to divert what could become a failed project. I said, "The people you have made available for this effort have no stake in its success or failure since they will be gone by the time the result takes place. Moreover, they know that this project is the only reason they are still here. As such, it is in their best interest to lengthen the project time as much as possible. If we reassign a few key people, though, we can still have a successful outcome."

Despite my formal warning, nothing changed. The result was just as we predicted: catastrophic. The client experienced major issues delivering their maintenance services because their spare part inventory management processes were not adequately prepared for the change.

The final piece of the mobilization phase is to assess the potential ways by which you could fulfil the strategic goals, evaluating them against the resources you have and the reality of the situation and defining the way forward. In doing so, you may identify gaps (as I did in this inventory management project) that need to be filled before you can effectively deliver your solution.

Identifying Possible Plans

Before you begin any journey, you need to have a plan. That is, you need to chart your course and be specific about how things will happen along the way. Your first step is to break down the major project components into manageable pieces. Although templates or general project plans may be helpful, no single methodology can account for all the variables in the change of an organization. You cannot and will not find a ready-made tool that spells out every action item required to reach your destination.

Mr. Schmidt, for example, depends on his consultants too much. He relies on the firm's experience and expertise but does not consciously realize that he knows his own company and its business better than the consultants ever will. Although they can certainly apply their knowledge base and experience from other outsourcing projects, they do not have the perspective necessary to customize their ready-made tools to his company's particular situation.

When the fragrance company Firmenich hired me, I was prepared to draw on my degree in natural science. But, the more I worked with the company, the more I realized that chemistry was just a manufacturing process for them; they did not sell chemistry per se. When their would-be customer picks up a bottle of perfume, they do not think: "Oh, I always wanted to wear this particular organic compound on my body." No, they think: "Oh, this reminds of the holiday evening I spent with my husband three years ago at that inn with the smell of magnolias in the air."

But, when I worked with the engineers at the train manufacturer Bombardier, their mindset was completely different. They did not sell emotions or memories, but rather quality precision. The market, the mindset and the method were completely different.

As the consultant in these vastly different projects, I could bring my expertise in change management to bear and act as a catalyst, but my clients' counterparts were the subject matter experts on their companies and industries. The particular nature of each company, its different aims, its unique restrictions and advantages and each initiative's specifics all underscore the need for an adaptive methodology that takes its cues from the underlying specifics of each.

You (or, in Mr. Schmidt's case, the consultants) simply cannot use the same plan and approach that proved successful in a previous initiative. Although you may draw lessons from that plan and even use some of the same tools, there is no substitute for the first-hand knowledge of the people in your coalition. With continual feedback from all sides, your plan will necessarily adapt and evolve until you have the right approach for your company.

Once you identify those components (no small feat in itself), you need to establish a realistic time frame, linking each major achievement to a milestone date. You must continually evaluate the potential gaps between your available resources and your stated objectives. When you establish those milestones, go back to your original parameters to see whether you have the time and budget to achieve them. Although it may sound elementary, I have witnessed many project leaders set a final date of delivery and project scope without adapting their vision of delivery to the available budget and other resources. Effective change leaders take the opposite tack: They begin with the budget and available resources and then work backward from there.

Also, you should add some cushion to the estimated costs and required time frame. Inevitably, something will go wrong. As I said previously, nothing ever goes according to plan. But as US General Dwight Eisenhower said: "In preparing for battle I have found that plans are useless, but planning is indispensable."

Building on Your Strengths

Any successful change initiative builds on existing strengths and capabilities. That is, the plan organically arises from the nature of the organization. However, I see plenty of initiatives fail because the sponsors and project managers approach it from the other way around: They decide on a plan and then try to force the company to adapt to it.

Mr. Schmidt, for example, should consider what existing people he has access to who can support the transition to an outsourced accounts payable (A/P) department, as well as who will manage the outsourced vendor once the transition is completed. By planning for that outcome beforehand, he can begin preparing someone for that role. Otherwise, he may accidentally create a position he cannot fill internally. He would then have to scramble to hire someone from outside the company at the last minute who may not be familiar with the company. Also, he may not have the experience to effectively oversee a newly outsourced department that is still being established.

Although the ultimate plan of action will be yours to make, the process of creating it cannot be a unilateral one. As the change leader, it is not your responsibility to conceive of all possible solutions, foresee every potential challenge, and create a step-by-step execution. It is your responsibility to facilitate an environment in which your resources—at this point, the initiative's sponsors and your supporting team—can together develop the various alternatives to best achieve the goal.

This is where your ability to mediate between opposing viewpoints will be severely put to the test. You must continually solicit ideas and advice from your coalition—from the chief executive officer to the customer service representative—without alienating or isolating any one party. Although each individual of your coalition can provide individual input, they may not have the perspective (or simply the time) to evaluate others' input. As a result, it is your responsibility to objectively judge which ideas to pursue and which to stop putting time toward—all while keeping the ideas' originators motivated about supporting you.

Seeing and Filling the Gaps

As I alluded to earlier—and as I tried to accomplish with the recalcitrant MD I mentioned in Chapter 4, you can acquire resources additional to the ones you were provided. You do not have to accept the limitations of your current team members to be the limits within which you must work. As a leader, take the initiative to look beyond what you have. Try to see and fill the gaps. Attempt to acquire the additional resources or skills you may need as you create a plan around delivering the strategic initiative.

When my clients are marshalling their own team, I encourage them to look across department silos to find potential subject matter experts. For example, Mr. Schmidt might have a number of accounting personnel tasked with supporting him, but if he plans to outsource the A/P department to another country—presumably involving the transfer of digital files—do you not think he should have a representative from information technology (IT) involved? Because a number of roles will change and potentially dozens of people will be laid off, should not someone from human resources (HR) be on board in helping to design the transition?

Such a lack of understanding and coordination between departments poses a problem that can lead to disastrous oversights. We had a close call of this nature with our client's product-numbering system. After gathering information from marketing, sales, operations and elsewhere, we had formulated a strategic plan to implement the new system. At that point, one employee on the team said, "Well, I guess we should talk to supply chain management, too."

Quite worried, I said: "The supply chain isn't represented in the operations people we have on our team?"

"Oh, no, they're two different parts of the company," he said.

We immediately brought in a supply chain expert. He pointed out that, even without having to check, he knew that the product relabeling would result in substantial tax increases in Turkey and Argentina, to name just two countries. The paperwork would show that one product had been imported but another one exported, leading the authorities to determine that substantial production had taken place and would be subject to extra taxation. Eventually, this would require a total change of processes, so much, in fact, that the expected revenue increases would be eclipsed by the cost.

It was fortunate the employee spoke up in time to avert disaster. We were able to completely restructure our approach—with a representative of the supply chain sitting at the table—and implement a workable solution that, although not as comprehensive as the original, was the best alternative.

In brainstorming potential solutions with your coalition, continually evaluate the potential gaps you need to fill. Regardless of the direction Mr. Schmidt chooses to go, he will need to involve more departments than are currently represented in his coalition, namely, HR and IT. If he decides also to focus on streamlining A/P processes, he may need to hire process consultants to assist him.

Some obstacles are insurmountable. If you are tasked with spearheading a new product into Asia, you may want to roll out a massive advertising campaign. However, if the cost of doing so exceeds your expected revenues, then your corporate sponsor will be reluctant to allocate the budget. Because that option is closed, you will have to find another way to achieve the goal (which may include redefining the goal).

On the other hand, your coalition might identify that a grassroots marketing campaign would be ideal, even if it pushes back your expected delivery date of six months. However, there is simply no way to execute it against the current schedule. In that case, you could go back to upper management, present a compelling case, and acquire an additional two months of time.

Although you may have established parameters to work within, you are not necessarily restricted to those parameters. When there is a major gap between your available resources (be it people, time, or money) and the reality you want to achieve, the only way forward is to get the additional resources you need to fill the gap. You may be given additional resources or your resources may be withdrawn. You can ask for resources or renegotiate the scope of your project altogether. You can decide to invest in training your resources.

The process of change is, in itself, a process of continual change. The proposed plan to achieve your business change must necessarily be a fluid one, hence the need for an adaptive approach.

Being a change leader means more than just managing a project. It means seeing what is not there, blazing new trails, and widening the realm of possibility.

Challenge Questions

1. What activities have you scheduled to fill the gaps in the organization, the procedures and the structure?
2. Will the affected employees be able to deal with the speed of the implementation?

3. Has your implementation plan been adapted to your company's specific situation?
4. How will each of your team members support the initiative?
5. Have you effectively communicated the roles and responsibilities to the project team?

PHASE **II**

CRUSADE

Designing the Solution

At the start of the crusading phase, you should have:

- the support of your coalition
- an aligned vision and a starting point
- the resources necessary to execute according to that plan

Once you have decided on a viable solution, you switch from focussing on how to achieve the desired change to how to define the proposed solution. Even as you further plan and implement your initiative, you must continually expand your circle of influence. This includes your coalition—your initiative's sponsors, key stakeholders and your core implementation team—but that circle needs to grow to encompass ambassadors, change agents and other such group influencers who can sow the seeds of change at all levels.

Let us review the four recurring questions you always need to ask throughout your initiative and the answers specifically for this phase:

■ *Why* am I crusading?
  To identify the specific business changes required in the organization

■ *Who* am I crusading to?
  Project sponsors
  Key stakeholders
  Implementation team members
  Representatives of all affected stakeholder groups
  Ambassadors, evangelists, change agents, superusers and so on

■ *What* am I crusading for?
  To design new organizational structures and processes

■ *Where* will crusading take me?
  To effective implementation of the plan

Chapter 6

Embarking
on the Journey

জলরে ধারে দাড়ঁয়িে জলরে পানে চেয়ে চেয়ে সাগর পাড়ঁদয়ো
যায়না।

You can't cross the sea merely by standing and star-
ing at the water.

—Rabindranath Tagore

Mr. Schmidt took a deep breath and began his
presentation.

"Thank you all for the opportunity to apprise
you of the outsourcing project. It seems like just a
few days ago we met in this very room to discuss
the viability of the initiative. Today, I am proud to
demonstrate the progress we have already made."

He stole a quick glance at Monsieur Valery,
who nodded encouragement and then continued,
"As you can see from this slide, the consultants we
hired have brought a well-developed methodology on board and used their predesigned process

templates to quickly roll out the outline of a new structure. In this slide, you can see that for the past few weeks, all the status reports we have collected from various departments are in the green—everyone is making progress at the rate they should for us to meet our established milestones."

After quickly going through a few other macroindicators, Mr. Schmidt wrapped up his presentation. "I have been very impressed by the consultants so far. With the company's focus on implementing best practice, our internal team has experienced minimal disruption. We have had some internal resistance, but I think that's to be expected in this type of project. Altogether, we are on track to deliver the project's objectives on time and on budget."

The CIO [chief information officer] spoke up: "This is all very impressive, Schmidt. I wish we would have found this consultancy when we were doing our outsourcing project!"

Mr. Schmidt flashed him a smile. "Thank you. They have been great to work with so far."

The CEO [chief executive officer] said, "This is all very good, but what problems have you encountered? What issues are you monitoring to make sure things go according to plan?"

"We have accounted and planned for everything we can directly control. I think the biggest challenge we face is eliciting support from the affected teams—namely, A/P [accounts payable]. The rest of the finance personnel largely seem to be okay, knowing that there won't be much required of them. Everyone else will see little change. So, if we can just figure out how to motivate our A/P teams, we should be okay," Mr. Schmidt said.

The CEO said, "I understand many of the in-country A/P processes differ from ours?"

Mr. Schmidt nodded. "That's right. Between the companies we've bought over the last few years and our expansion into Asia, we haven't been able to keep a standard approach. We've let the local teams administer the A/P functions as they see fit, as long as they send us the information in the formats we need here at corporate."

The CEO continued to press: "And, you've planned for transitioning from their procedures to a company-wide standard?"

"We are designing that transition, yes," Mr. Schmidt said.

"You know what they say, Schmidt: 'The devil's in the details.' And there a lot of details on the table."

"Yes there are," he said. "But we also have a lot of talent sitting at that table," he said.

Only after you have aligned your vision of change with your sponsors and

- earned the buy-in of your key stakeholders,
- assembled your implementation team,
- firmly decided on a course of action,
- created a transition plan that has been thoroughly vetted by your coalition
- and secured the additional resources needed to implement such a plan

are you finally ready to begin acting on your plans.

This is usually an exciting time. The future is bright, the budget seems sufficient, the intricate details appear trifling, and there are no storms on the horizon. Mr. Schmidt feels this way right now. He is happy about the structure the consultants have proposed and the process templates they have prepared. But, as we say in Germany, *Papier ist geduldig* ("paper is patient").

Having a written plan does not make it real any more than a line between two points on a map reveals the journey.

Despite communicating with everyone, despite the buy-in of your coalition, despite having everything down in black and white, you cannot flip the autopilot switch, then sit back and relax as everyone executes according to the plan. As the change leader, you must lead change. Leadership not only is about creating a vision but also is about actively managing the elements that will bring about the desired transformation.

Designing the Change

In a presentation to a group of directors for a construction material manufacturer, I showed a slide that had random dots scattered across a white background.

"What do you see?" I asked.

After a few people hazarded their guesses, I switched to the next slide that showed the same dots, but they were connected to represent the Pegasus star constellation. Once I explained how to trace the constellation, they could all see the outline of the winged horse of Greek mythology.

I said, "That's how the project might feel to your people right now. They can see lots of dots, but they may not see how to connect them. From where they're sitting right now, they don't understand how each isolated element relates to the big picture. Until they do, they cannot imagine it all coming together in something as majestic as a mythical horse."

By the end of the mobilization phase, you have decided on a plan of action—your team's proposal of how to deliver the desired strategic results. Crusading is about gaining additional support for your proposed solution and about filling in the blanks. You hold a map that has your current position and your proposed route to your destination, but that is all your map reveals. You must finish filling in the details before you can get under way.

As the person at the helm, you cannot possibly oversee the execution of every detail (not in a project of any substantial size, anyway). And, micromanaging your resources and forcing incessant status reports so you can remain in control rarely results in successful, lasting results.

You need to give your team the big picture (connect the dots for them, as in the Pegasus example) and provide clear direction. Your people will then be able to connect the dots and provide the details of the change. To achieve real, tangible results, you need people to work on real, tangible activities. They need to stay in the communication loop, they need clear goals (measurable, if possible), and they need clear feedback on their individual and collective efforts.

You want to foster a working environment in such a way that the members of your team can interact with each other as well as the other members of your coalition. They need to exchange ideas, apprise each other of their progress, devise workarounds for unforeseen issues and find new ways to work together. The more nodes of activity and the more information exchanged, the more quickly potential resource gaps or new issues can bubble up to you.

Expanding your coalition is critical to your success. By being in close contact with people represented throughout the organization, you will have an open line of communication with potentially affected employees who can bring such issues to your attention. The faster these issues reach you, the faster you can react to prevent or mitigate them.

With Firmenich, we explicitly created a change advisory board composed of stakeholders from throughout the project whose responsibility was to help us (the implementation team) identify the potential impact of the change initiative. The members of the advisory board took our plans and processes back to their local sites and considered how the changes would affect their own roles and functions—long before the new structure was ever set in motion.

The critical concept here is to involve other stakeholders not only in the high-level design (such as whether to outsource the A/P department versus consolidating it) but also in planning the transition to achieve it. In changing any aspect of an organization, you should plan for how others will shoulder their new responsibilities and how they might respond to the new demands placed on them. Some people may quickly embrace change, but plenty will be slow to come on board.

Be Ready to Adapt Your Plan

To use our analogy of a journey, some leaders plan on what their followers should do when they arrive at their destination, but they forget about the voyage itself. They become so wrapped up in planning what the outcome of their initiative should look like that they forget to adequately plan for what that transformation entails. An effective change plan addresses the need to restructure existing processes, but it must also address the need for an effective transition from the current processes to the new ones.

I was hired once to work with a company that was in the middle of executing a worldwide project. Upper management did a superb job of communicating with their global managers. They had identified a new organizational structure and made sure their managers understood what they were doing and why. They were very good at disseminating the message, holding multiple conference calls with representatives throughout the departments to thoroughly discuss what the change meant for them, what would be expected, how the new structure would work and so on. The problem was that they spent so much time focussing on where they were going that they forgot about what it looked like in the interim.

The executives set a target delivery date for four weeks. In Asia, this posed no problem. The changes happened according to their timetable. But, in most of their European offices, human resources raised a red flag. Substantial changes to individuals' job descriptions require a lengthy approval process, including consultations with the local works council. In some cases, the company had to renegotiate entire positions, replete with new job descriptions and even new contracts. What was supposed on paper to take four weeks took more than six months in reality.

After having told their workers of the coming changes in January, it took them until July to finalize their decisions and execute them. Those additional months created a negative environment for the affected employees. They were frustrated about not knowing the fate of their jobs and what the end results of those ensuing negotiations and endless rounds of approvals would be. Consequently, productivity fell as their morale was sapped.

Your initial plans must clarify the key aspects of the project. Who are the people with the responsibility for handling various tasks? How will different stakeholders' roles and responsibilities change? Where will the resources (e.g., time, personnel and budget) come from? What activities and processes will be affected during the transition as those resources are diverted to your project? What activities and processes will be permanently affected when you have fully implemented your plan?

Failing to account for the major changes in your organization will negatively impact your success. How do you prepare an organization for change? What communication, training, and involvement activities should you plan? How can you predict all the ways that the organization and its processes will be affected? How do you ensure that everyone connected to the changes will be adequately informed? How will you involve others in changing the company?

As one executive in a company with hundreds or even thousands of employees, you cannot possibly see all the links between your initiative's proposed changes and the ripple effects they can have throughout your organization. For example, my firm was hired to manage a particular component of a much larger change project. In the course of managing my portion of the work, I flew to a distant (and freezing) branch office in Canada. I spent a few days with the local employees running through the company's new strategy to provide more in-depth communication than the team had received via e-mail.

In discussing the implications, one person said, "You know, I wonder if we'll still be here in a year's time? Listening to you, it sounds like the services we provide won't be needed by the end of this project."

I had not heard of any suggestions to cut their office, so I focussed the discussion on the objectives at hand, stressing the positive aspects and how they could become part of the new organization. But, that employee's instincts were correct. Their company had not, in fact, planned for how the transition would affect their faraway Canadian branch office. After implementation, upper management realized the office was superfluous.

The primary executive in charge wanted to keep the long-standing employees. Of course, after the change, there was no place for them to go. He delayed making a decision for almost a year. Eventually, he was forced to make a choice and necessarily had to lay them off. But, that year of indecision and uncertainty was painful for the employees at the branch office and harmful to the morale and productivity of the other people they influenced.

Reasons like these are exactly why I employ an adaptive methodology. To be an effective change leader, it is crucial that your plan of execution evolves to address the new and unforeseen circumstances that arise. This executive, in contrast, was unprepared to deal with the situation when things did not go according to plan. They never do.

Shoring Up Your Original Support

Once you have a plan for execution (even if you know it will necessarily evolve), you need to revisit the key people in your coalition to affirm their buy-in on the clarified plan of execution. Some people are only too willing to give their support when the project consists only of an ideal outcome and some vague ideas on how to achieve it. When the details of exactly how you will go about accomplishing the change begin to coalesce, their support may begin to evaporate.

Just as you began with the initiative's sponsors, so should you begin there again. When you do, remember to continually communicate what is in it for them. How will your plan benefit your sponsors? Will it make them look good in front of their respective superiors, be they the C-suite (the different chief executives), the board of directors or shareholders? Will it allow them to achieve their own performance goals? Will it take tasks off their desk and make their jobs easier?

You may need to break your master plan down into even smaller, more digestible steps. By concentrating on a series of small wins, you may be able to instil a sense of accomplishment and positive momentum for everyone involved. People like being on the winning team: The more they feel like they (and you) are winning, the more support and buy-in you should earn.

Converting Others into Your Evangelists

Aim for about 10% of the affected people to be aware of the initiative and support your efforts before you even begin to implement the solution. The more people who do so, the better chance you have of succeeding. In the previous advisory board story, not only did the people in it help us design a more comprehensive solution and then help us design an effective transition, but also their active participation turned them into our ambassadors in their respective departments. They became our "evangelists of change," if you will, leveraging their relationships with their peers and co-workers to earn their buy-in. Because they were invested in the solution's design, they took ownership of its outcome.

The more influential each of your supporters is, the more they can help you garner additional support. In expanding your circle of influence, target these influencers. Even though they may not have any additional skill sets or perspectives you need, they affect a disproportionately larger segment of people. By making them part of your coalition, you can turn them into superevangelists. When it comes time to roll out your project to its full extent, they can help pave the way.

The more evangelists you have on your side, the faster your message will be disseminated throughout the company. This way, an initiative that starts out with a small group can quickly scale up, eventually growing to include a majority of the affected stakeholders supporting and working toward the project's success.

Challenge Questions

1. Does your team have the required information to work on designing the change?
2. Have you identified individual transition plans for the key stakeholder groups?
3. Have you started identifying and involving your evangelists (that is, the people who will influence the broader organization to accept the change)?
4. Are you still in contact with your sponsors, updating them on your progress and checking on their ongoing support?
5. Are you regularly adapting your plan based on changes in the business environment?

Chapter 7

Captaining, Despite Shortages and Scurvy

The wind and the waves are always on the side of the ablest navigators.

—Edward Gibbon

Mr. Schmidt reached for the ringing phone. "Hello?"

"Hi, Schmidt. How was Morocco? Decide on a company yet?" the managing consultant asked.

"Not yet. I did a site visit of the four companies we identified—but I must tell you that I have my reservations," Mr. Schmidt said.

"Let's hear them."

"Well, they all have the capabilities to read and scan invoices, but here are the issues. The start-up we looked at doesn't have the bandwidth to handle the kind of financial files we're going to be transferring back and forth around the world every day. I talked to some local clients of that family-run company, and they have a horrible reputation for customer service—as in, you can't get them to return a call unless you call the owner at his house. But, they offer the best price of everybody. The big company runs on an older system that is incompatible with ours; they would have to convert every single file they got before they could even open it. I'm worried about file corruption. And, the last company doesn't have the security protocols we require. They're willing to upgrade—if we'll foot the bill."

Mr. Schmidt sighed. "We could possibly work through all of these issues—if we were so inclined, if we had the time, and if there were no other options."

The consultant said, "I hate to be the bearer of bad news, but we have trouble on the home front, too."

"Oh?"

"I'm having some real issues with your project team. I mean, they knew that this was going to be a big project, right? I can't seem to get through to them that they have to put in the extra time. They're complaining that they don't have time on top of their everyday responsibilities. For instance, one guy absolutely refuses to stay late for overseas phone calls. Says he doesn't want to be late for dinner. Can you believe it?"

Mr. Schmidt ran his hand through his hair. "I hear what you're saying. There has been a lot of resistance to this project from the start. Everyone that I'm working with was 'volunteered' to be on my team, and they're not happy about it."

He paused. "But surely you've encountered this before? With your other consulting projects? Is there something else you're having an issue with?"

"Actually, yes. I don't know if I made this clear at the beginning of the project, but I depend on you to enforce the project requirements with others. I've attempted to contact the regional finance directors to set up a meeting with each. I can't get half of them to respond to my repeated e-mails or my phone calls—not to even discuss the agenda, much less the meeting. I copied you on all of them as a subtle way of asking for your help. I appreciate your trust in my abilities, but you have to herd your own people. All of them," the consultant said.

Mr. Schmidt sighed again. "All right, I'll take responsibility for that. I'll see what I can do."

After they hung up, Mr. Schmidt turned to his wife. "Everything started out so great. I don't know what went wrong."

She said, "Well, I guess there are some things you just can't outsource."

When we left Mr. Schmidt in Chapter 6, it seemed like everything was running smoothly with his project. With little effort, you could imagine him giving himself a congratulatory pat on the back. Before this phone call, Mr. Schmidt was in the honeymoon phase: in love with his idea, seeing the bright future ahead for himself and blind to the shortcomings of his plan.

Perhaps you might even say this is like the feeling at the beginning of a new relationship or marriage. We are so infatuated with our vision of how wonderful things will be that we fail to fully anticipate the challenges that lie ahead. At the beginning of an initiative, when much of the plan has yet to be implemented, it is easy to feel this false sense of security.

Now, of course, his little daydream looks like it is crashing down around him. He is beginning to see that there might be a lot more work involved than he realized. He has overestimated the extent to which he can rely on the consultancy to lead the change. Also, because he was enthusiastic about the project, he assumed that others—or, at least the upper-level finance directors—would be equally enthusiastic.

Big initiatives always end up looking more like hell than heaven. Regardless of the size or scope, your change initiative will encounter problems. You will find unexpected twists in some stakeholders' perspectives. Some people will suddenly be vague about their activities or how committed they are. Some problems may be minor, like simply getting people to communicate with their counterparts in inconvenient time zones. Some may be major, like having your budget suddenly cut in half.

But, the complaint I hear more often and more loudly from managers is about the quality of the people involved—especially their employees. One client of mine, a chief executive officer (CEO), had an annual meeting during which he berated his top managers for failing to support some of the company's key initiatives. He told them: "I am surrounded by incompetence!" After such public humiliation, the managers redoubled their visible efforts. Who wouldn't? In a way, the CEO did solve his problem: immediate and measurable progress was made on his pet projects.

But, all he really did was to trade one problem for a much bigger one. His lack of tact and respect insulted his managers and everyone else in the company. His speech rippled throughout the company and seriously deteriorated the company's culture. Some executives even confided in me that they were thinking of looking for another place of employment where their contributions would be valued.

People do not "lack skills" or "have poor skills." They have skills. It just may be that those skills are not suited to the task at hand. You can berate them for not being in possession of what they need. Or, you could help them acquire what they lack.

Few employees truly want to do a bad job. The vast majority I have seen and worked with sincerely want to do a great job. In fact, they usually do the best they can with what they have. The issue is the gap between the skill level they have and the skill level they need.

If you begin thinking about how poor a job someone is doing, stop to ask yourself if the employee's motivation is the problem or if it stems from their lack of practice and experience? Instead of trying to motivate them to do better, try equipping them to do better. Coaching, training, mentoring, educating and making other resources available might be the real answer to the perceived deficiency.

Managing Project People

As explored in the chapter on taking stock of ship and crew, some excellent employees do not make excellent project members. They may be a great fit for their particular position, they may be comfortable because they have done the rote processes for so long, or they may simply enjoy the predictable nature of their tasks. Whatever the reason, some of these same model professionals do not automatically translate into model project members.

As the leader of the initiative, you have the responsibility to recognize the potential gaps in the skill sets and mindsets between the person assigned to your team and the tasks you have assigned them.

Moreover, you have the responsibility to fill the gap. That may come from working one-on-one with the person, from providing the training they need, or even from shuffling personnel around to match their abilities to a task better suited for them. Depending on their personality, you may need to provide a different level of structure—either more rigid or more flexible—than you are used to providing in other instances. Some of your team members will thrive by having elaborate guidelines, forms and a complex project plan. Others work better in a relaxed atmosphere where they do not feel stifled and are free to pursue their tasks on their own.

One of your biggest challenges will be to balance the different requirements of your diverse team, recognizing the signs that you need to modify your approach to managing your people. When individuals begin to slip on meeting their stated objectives, it may be a sign that they need more clarity, a different management style, more information, or simply some feedback.

At this point in your initiative, it is important to employ the crucial leadership skills covered in Chapter 2.

Modelling the Change

Every manager says they care for their employees, but I remember one in particular who truly demonstrated this. He had to let about a hundred people in his division go. The remaining employees were understandably scared about their own job security in the midst of such layoffs.

He took an entire day out of his incredibly busy schedule to have face-to-face meetings with those who were left. In small groups, he asked them to voice their worries and fears. He took the time to truly listen to what each of them said. Although he did not have all the answers to their questions, he did accomplish two important things: He acknowledged their concerns and showed that he cared about them.

Like this manager, you have to walk the walk. Your message is credible only if you act on it. Being a role model is primarily about being genuine in your approach. That is, your people need to trust you.

A good example is the time when, with Deloitte, I worked with three C-suite executives (aka chief executives) who wanted some high-level training in the new ERP (enterprise resource planning) system. Many people throughout the company were resisting the switch. To allay these fears and demonstrate their commitment to the change, the executives each took a half day to better learn the system. This occurred despite leading a 15,000-employee organization and despite the fact that they would never use the ERP in their own day-to-day activities.

On the other hand, I had another project for which many of the upper-level executives rejected attending twenty-minute trainings, arguing that they would never need to use the new information technology tool. They did not grasp the idea that their attendance would have shown how important the new process was for the rest of the company. They had a chance to be role models. Instead, they just demonstrated how unimportant they thought the new approach was.

What kind of role model would you be if you were a captain in the army? Would you be one of those leaders who sent soldiers in, saying, "Oh, don't worry. It's perfectly safe!" Or, would you be the one leading the charge?

The same is true for change. You have to be the first one to embrace it. If your company decides to abolish single offices, you have to be one of the first to move into the new open office floor plan—not the last. If your boss gives you the task of implementing a new collaboration tool to support global communication, you have to actively use it in your interactions with others. If you trust your own change initiative, walking the walk should come naturally.

The biggest challenge in being a role model is showing consistency and trust. At the beginning of the change, there is no momentum. It requires a tremendous effort on your part to get the ball rolling and persuading others to help you roll it. There are not many opportunities to be a real role model.

But, here in the crusading phase, modelling the change is more about being out in front, demonstrating that you are fully committed to the vision and its successful execution.

Motivating the Change

In times of stress and difficulties—that is, during the entire time you are working to implement the change plan—you will feel the urge to micromanage your team. This is normal. Many leaders feel that because they are responsible for the outcome of the project, they must stay on top of every detail. As problems arise, they automatically take the reins so that they can better guide and control the execution.

If you do this, every person under you will feel the effects. They will sense that you do not trust them and that you are looking for problems to address. This can easily devolve into a witch hunt, looking for minor mistakes and tracing the blame instead of focussing on the big picture. In these situations, people start spending less time achieving real accomplishments and more time covering their ass.

In times of adversity, your challenge is to keep a cool head and to continue to support individuals in their development. Inclusion and participation are some of the best tools to motivate and engage your people. Think of kids on a soccer team. What motivates them more? Worrying about their coaches complaining that are not practicing enough? Thinking about the five euros their parents promised them for scoring a goal? Or, feeling pride in scoring points for their team and moving into a higher league?

Your team members are not children, but their basic motivators are similar. A pat on the shoulder is short-lived, but identifying with their responsibilities, working with others and achieving a common vision will stay with them far longer.

That is not to say that rewards and recognition are not important. They are; they just should not stand alone. I am always surprised to meet people I worked with on change initiatives and discover that they do not remember the great presentation we had on the vision for the change or the good team workshops we had on the new processes. Instead, they talk about the great Christmas party we threw just for the coalition members or the sightseeing event we organized after reaching a key milestone.

People are people. Not everyone is motivated by the same incentives. For some, emotional rewards elicit more support than the tangible ones. On the other hand, some people appreciate the more material rewards. Still others simply want recognition and appreciation. The key is to take the time to understand the individual motivations of each of your employees.

Shaping the Change

We once worked with a CEO who we only belatedly learned was also a procrastinator. He was great at starting new projects and embracing the big picture. He did a good job in the mobilizing phase of genuinely persuading his upper-level managers to support his new initiatives. But, once we began moving into the crusading phase, he got lost in the details.

When we first began working with him, I loved the fact that whenever I was recommending a way forward, he would listen intently and enthusiastically nod. I took his body language as tacit agreement. It took me some time to figure out that this was just his way of signalling me to continue talking—not that he was ready to act.

He would take the idea and let it ripen, and ripen, and ripen, until it was almost rotten. He waited so long that either the problems solved themselves or had become moot. This worked for him until his company began posting major losses.

At that point, he was forced to start making definitive decisions, but he was paralyzed by the thought of making the wrong ones. I took the opportunity to help him sift through the mountain of problems he faced and apply the Pareto principle: to focus on resolving the 20% of the problems that would deliver 80% of the desired results and to postpone resolving the time-consuming remainder. He would necessarily make some mistakes, but he would also make some successful decisions. He would have to take the good with the bad.

It is fine to have an open mind to different opinions, but at some point, you have to act at the risk of being wrong. Previously, we talked about the pitfalls of micromanaging your team as a motivator, but that does not mean that you should remove yourself entirely, as this procrastinator did.

When you start encountering adversity and issues you have to proactively address them. You have to be clear about what you expect from the chief stakeholders, and you must take the lead in adapting your plans as the need arises. You have to instil confidence in times of uncertainty by giving individuals clear direction and vision. Your leadership will define what form the change will take.

Being a shaper means being clear on the way forward, being able to explain to others how they will transition from one situation to another or from one process to another. Of course, there will be gray areas and places where you simply have to guess which option is best. You cannot always avoid these situations.

Regardless, though, the message you need to get across here is: "I know where we are, where we are going, and together we will find a way to get there."

Mediating the Change

When you try to change people or an entire organization, you will encounter a multitude of rejections. If you do not deliberately and successfully extend your circle of influence to include the right people and stakeholder groups, you will undoubtedly encounter major resistance—from critical gate-keepers, from peers, from subordinates and from all those affected by the changes. Some issues might just be individual ones, linked to power, social hierarchy or self-interest. However, some resistance might be well founded and, if addressed adequately, can help you avoid major pitfalls.

I have seen change leaders wait until the populating phase of a project before reaching out to an affected stakeholder group for the first time. By then, the rumours had spread and resistance had taken a foothold. Even after the changes were fully implemented, all the groups had reported as being in compliance and the executive had declared the project a success, many individuals continued to use their old tools and processes. They never bought in to the idea before the implementation, so why should they buy in afterward? Resistance does not magically appear or magically disappear. It is like an avalanche: You must react and respond early, before it has time to build up overwhelming momentum.

Sometimes, resistance is emotionally based. Perhaps a person fears getting out of their comfort zone or resents being given more work. Often, though, resistance is a rational response. If someone does not see the need for change or disagrees with the solution, they may try to block the project. Also, if an employee does not know how to effectively interact with a new tool or how to be productive in the process, the employee may resist. Last but not least, people may resist because there is a real problem—your plan may have not addressed a real need, the tools may be substantially flawed, or the structure may leave a serious gap in operations. It could be that some people see that you do not have the requisite budget or buy-in from upper management. Because they believe your project will ultimately fail, why should they invest their time and energy?

Because resistance is so often rooted in such sensible perspectives, you should always try to uncover the real reason behind a stakeholder's reluctance to buy in to your vision for change.

You must also fear the lack of resistance. I have personally witnessed only one instance in which there was no opposition to the new change proposal—and it resulted in disaster. I was working with the regional managing directors of a media manufacturer to streamline their supply chain organization. Shortly before I began, upper management had declared a strategic goal for their sales department: They wanted their salespeople to sell as many products as possible to retail stores. To support this goal, each salesperson's bonus was tied directly to their sales numbers. The bigger the retailers' orders were, the bigger the salesperson's bonus was.

The salespeople performed flawlessly. Gross sales sailed through the roof and, with them, the salespeople's bonuses. Everyone was excited and happy, and the sales initiative was viewed as a great success. Only later did the problems begin to show up.

Retailers began returning the vast majority of the products. This, of course, was an enormous problem because every return wasted the resources that went into its production plus the costs of delivery, return and destruction. As the returns mounted, leadership began to worry.

When they investigated, they discovered the fatal flaw in their plan: The new bonus system did not account for returns. The retailers' contracts stipulated that they paid only for the products bought by the consumers; all others could be returned to the manufacturer at no cost to the retailers. On the other hand, the salespeople's bonuses were based solely on gross sales. The sales initiative created a loophole wherein the salespeople did not look to identify each retailer's real needs. The salespeople heaped products on the retailers, ensuring them that they could return the unsold merchandise later.

The whole initiative succeeded only in putting more products on the shelves—whether shoppers actually bought them or not. As the Americans say, they shot themselves in the foot.

The company's clue that something was amiss should have been the total lack of resistance. Not one single salesperson raised any kind of objection to the new bonus system. In your own project, look for resistance—but also look for its absence.

By the same token, let me say that someone continuously challenging the change does not necessarily mean that they resist it. In one of our projects, one manager in particular would pop in two or three times a day to question the team's decisions, play devil's advocate, and generally meddle to the point of disruption. Others referred to him as "a pain in the neck."

Yet, in the end, he was our biggest champion. Because he had been actively involved, he had proven to himself that we had an actionable plan to execute and knew exactly how the project would affect his department. He evangelized on our behalf, overcoming many other managers' resistance who had not been as involved. His apparent resistance was simply his way of doing his due diligence.

Communicating the Change

The core of good leadership in a change project is the ability to communicate well. You cannot fulfil the four other aspects of leadership without this skill (see Figure 7.1).

I am not talking about holding motivational speeches in front of thousands of people. This is about the ability to listen, inspire and provide clarity. It means being able to interact respectfully with people with different goals and motivations. It means being able to be effectively understood in your other roles as a shaper, mediator, motivator and role model.

Communication is a two-way street. As a leader, one of your key skills is listening. In listening, you can learn what is

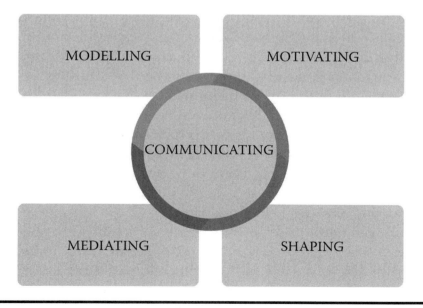

Figure 7.1 Effective communication. Communication is shaped not only by spoken words but also by adhering to the behaviour you wish to see in your employees as well as involving them from the beginning.

important for your counterpart, what goals they are aiming for, and what their worries are. Listening can be hard, as it means we need to be patient and not force our own message on the other person. Too often, people start preparing their answer while you are still talking—a sure sign they are not listening properly. If you want to make sure you really hear their message, allow some pauses in the discussion so both of you have time to absorb the other's points.

I know a CEO of a company with over 30,000 employees who strictly follows an open-door policy. This shows not only that he cares but also that he welcomes feedback, questions and ideas. He actively demonstrates that he is available and is not hiding behind a closed door.

To be credible, your communication needs to be genuine. When you are going through major change, you might not always be in a position to give out all the details of the restructuring (like the need for further layoffs), but if you lie once, your employees will not forget. Once your credibility is gone, how can your employees trust the other things you communicate? If you want to be perceived as a real leader, then people need to trust you. For that, you need to earn their respect—and that you can only achieve through honesty and empathy.

When talking about communication, we need also to address the different communication needs throughout the world. If you are not sure how a certain message will be perceived in India, Mexico or Sweden, cross-check with someone culturally knowledgeable who can help you avoid a misstep—perhaps an internal person, a local peer or a vendor with whom you have worked in the past.

You can never overcommunicate. It takes time for a message to stick. Plus, you are not the only person trying to get your ideas across. Small bits of information are more easily digestible than a full-blown communication pack. Through regularly distributing your key messages and methodically crafting a story for your transition, you will be able to strongly position your initiative in the minds of your stakeholders.

Challenge Questions

1. Do you understand the specific leadership needs of the various stakeholder groups?
2. What concrete examples can you identify of "walking the talk" and being a role model for the change?
3. What actions have you planned to motivate and inspire the affected employees?
4. Are you ready to make hard decisions and take clear-cut action to move the initiative forward?
5. How are you tackling the key resistance points?
6. How do you plan to address the different information needs?

Chapter 8

Surviving the Tempests

De vissers weten dat het zee gevaarlijk is en het storm is vreselijk, maar zij hebben nooit deze gevaren voldoende reden gevonden om aan wal te blijven.

The fishermen know that the sea is dangerous and the storm terrible, but they have never found these dangers sufficient reason for remaining ashore.

—Vincent Van Gogh

Mr. Schmidt stabbed his dinner and then silently gulped his wine. From across the table, his wife gave him a knowing look.

He sighed. "I'm just frustrated. It seems like as soon as something in this project starts going right, something else breaks. I hate to be insensitive, but why did Monsieur Valery have to have a heart attack?"

His wife smiled. "I'm sure he would have avoided it if he could."

"It's just—it just couldn't have happened at a worse time. After hiring a political analyst and looking at the legalities, Morocco doesn't seem like it's going to work out. The economic outlook doesn't look good and some execs are concerned about it being close to the unrest in North Africa. So, just when we're getting ready to find another site, my main backer has to back out—entirely! He won't be back to work for months."

He stabbed at his plate again and chewed in silence.

After a moment, his wife said, "But that's not the real problem, is it?"

He chewed some more. "No. It's his temporary replacement. Anna." He wrinkled his nose when he said it.

"I've met her at the Christmas parties before," she said. "She seemed nice."

"Well, you've never had her for a boss. It doesn't help that if Monsieur Valery doesn't come back, we'll both be vying for his job—and if this outsourcing project succeeds, it'll probably go to me."

"Ah—your rival as your boss. Yes, that could get complicated quickly. But, you've handled something like this before."

Mr. Schmidt pushed back from the table. "I guess I'm embarrassed. Now that Morocco is no longer a viable option, we have to start from scratch looking at another country. The CEO [chief executive officer] has granted us more time, but not more budget, which means I have to let the consultants go and do everything they did on my own now. I'm going to have to plead and beg for help from some of our branch offices and a couple of other departments. After seeing the consultants do it, I see how much work has to be done. I am not looking forward to it—especially with a supervisor who doesn't support me."

He paused. "It's like going back to being a salesperson again. I'm going to have to sell this project to procure some help from other managers. I didn't think I had to sell this because I had the backing of the CEO and CFO [chief financial officer]. But now . . ."

"But now what?" she asked.

"Now, it's just a lot more work than I planned, with a lot fewer resources than before."

"So, how will you begin?"

He chewed his lip. "I guess exactly where I began a few months ago—selling the idea of outsourcing to my boss. Only this time, it's a hard sell."

In one large system implementation in Belgium, the original project team included some 200 people. About 100 were internal employees, and the other 100 were external consultants. I was quite excited that we had so much support. For two years, we planned and executed with this wealth of talent.

Then, the company's financial fortunes changed, and the chief information officer (CIO) was forced to curtail the project. Almost overnight, half of the team was let go. We were down to 100 people. Then came another round of budget cuts. Once again, the project team was cut in half, leaving us with just 50 people. With only a fourth of the personnel left, we had to completely change the scope and nature of the project. Two years' worth of work went into the waste bin. The project started over from scratch. Shortly thereafter, almost all the external consultants were asked to leave, including me.

Instead of going home, though, I decided to give myself a much-needed vacation, so I went skiing in Austria. On the slopes, I received a phone call from the client asking if I could come back. They realized they still needed a

German-speaking consultant to help them finish the project. I stowed my skis and went back to their office.

I have shared this anecdote with a number of people whose reaction was, "How could you work in such an environment? Fired one day and hired the next? Having your budget cut in half, not once, but twice? Having to start over from scratch? How could you accomplish anything?"

Such chaos, uncertainty and suboptimal conditions are normal. They are the reality you will inevitably face as a change leader. It is not a question of if such things will happen, but when.

Some executives I have worked with, when faced with such adversity, impressively rose to the challenge. Others, faced with similar circumstances, became frustrated and overwhelmed. Some faced the problem head on; others simply gave up and gave in.

I cannot stress this enough: There will be real problems that will completely kill your initiative—if you let them. I advise my clients to actively look for problems. I counsel them to try to imagine what could possibly go wrong so that they can proactively address those situations. The English proverb says that "an ounce of prevention is worth a pound of cure." The solution is not necessarily to try to solve these problems outright, but to plan for them and mitigate them so that you stay on course.

In all the change projects I have led, managed, observed or studied over my entire career, I have seen only two initiatives that delivered the promised results more or less on time, more or less on budget. They had two things in common. For one, they both had a flexible plan that could accommodate and adapt to new challenges. Two, they included experienced support personnel who had participated in such projects before. But, the inclusion of these two elements cannot guarantee success any more than their absence might guarantee failure. The fact is that plenty of projects that experienced major hurdles turned out to be successful.

As long as everyone agrees on what needs to be achieved and how it should be done, all you need is enough time, support, and money to pull it off. Such scenarios are fantasies. The reality of life is that we must attempt to achieve optimal outcomes under suboptimal conditions.

The economy might collapse. The CEO might be replaced. The market could shift. Your customers could change. Something like this will inevitably happen.

The question is: What can you do—right now—to ensure success despite the presence of such tempests?

Contingency Planning

In a phrase, plan for these tempests using contingency planning. Managing the unexpected might seem impossible, but it is the trait of a true leader, as well as one of the key factors of success in a change initiative. You must constantly adapt to ever-changing conditions. In your own project, you might face economic, financial, organizational, legal, personal or even physical challenges, like Monsieur Valery.

I had an experience working for Deloitte in which the client's major sponsor died from a heart attack. Consequently, the client gave over the initiative entirely to the consultant team because we had all been working closely with the sponsor. This certainly was not ideal, but it was necessary to keep the project from falling apart. For this very reason, I always identify deputies for key stakeholders who can step in if we somehow lose the primary person. That way, regardless of whether the key stakeholders are incapacitated (in the case of a heart attack), leave the company to take another position or simply go on holiday, the initiative can continue to move forward.

What are the major risks to your own project? These will vary, depending on the scope of the strategic objective, your industry, the resources you have available and other situation-specific factors. You must draw not only on your experience, but also on your colleagues', sponsors' and stakeholders' experiences to identify such factors. Once you have identified the plausible scenarios, make contingency plans. Believe me, you would rather plan for a problem that never happens than face a problem you have never planned for.

In Mr. Schmidt's case, he runs the risk of interrupting payments to the company's vendors. Because this scenario could damage his company's relationship with its suppliers and his company's own internal operations, he should plan for such a disaster. If it were to happen, how would he deal with it? What options would he have?

Acrasio faced such a scenario in a warehouse management project when we assessed the risks of consolidating the administrative services of the company. In the event of a catastrophic failure, the employees were prepared to unplug their computers from the network and manually print and mail the physical documents needed to keep their operations running. It might seem like a simple solution, but trust me: When such a fiasco happens, you do not want to be scrambling to come up with a contingency plan; you want to be executing the contingency plan you already have.

These contingencies can influence the execution of the plan itself. Were I advising Mr. Schmidt, I would point out that he could avoid this particular scenario by first running a pilot with a small supplier account and managing his key suppliers' accounts internally until the outsourcing proved a success. Planning to do so not only would prove prudent but also could demonstrate to his superiors that he was taking the proper precautions and earning their trust (and, therefore, further buy-in).

Expecting the Worst

What is the number-one challenge you should expect? In a word: money. If your budget is restricted or cut during implementation, you would be foolish to believe that it will not jeopardize your delivery. In fact, about half of all the change projects I have worked with through McKinsey, Deloitte or Acrasio required us to push the delivery dates back and restructure our approach because of resource limitations. If a change in your resources or situation will delay the project's delivery by a month, then say so. It is better to disappoint your stakeholders earlier, to prepare them for what is to come, than to surprise them at the moment of truth. If you do not alter your project's deliverables to align with your revised resources, I can almost guarantee that you will fail.

Often, an insufficient budget or lack of needed resources reflects a lack of buy-in from upper executives. This might be the CEO, but it is often the other chief executives, such as the CFO or COO (chief operating officer). Although they may not have the final word on the resources available to you, having their support will make it easier to win the resources you need. This is especially true when you hit an unexpected obstacle and need help—help that they can give or that they might withhold because it pulls resources away from their own departments. Their opinion of your efforts will make the difference.

Do not be afraid to ask for additional resources. Curiously, I have found that it is easier to request a supplementary budget later in the project than to ask for the same amount at the outset. Many executives fear a larger financial commitment up front. As we discussed, people are often more willing to support an initiative that has demonstrated some success rather than support a similar effort when the outcome is still unknown.

People do not want to get on a ship that might sink.

Asking the Big Question Again

In the middle of implementing a solution, change leaders do not ask the big question again and overlook a critical element: periodically evaluating whether the change initiative is still necessary. They get so caught up in the project that they fail to realize the driving need may have changed or disappeared altogether.

As someone should have pointed out to Mr. Schmidt, the company's strategic objective was cost reduction—not outsourcing. After doing all the work to evaluate the accounts/payable (A/P) department's functions with an eye toward consolidating those tasks, what if the resulting standardization achieved the desired cost savings? Would Mr. Schmidt still need to pursue outsourcing? Of course not, but by now, he has become so enamoured with his idea that he has almost forgotten the reason he is doing it in the first place.

Many change projects are tied to milestones, and reporting concrete numbers provides a sense of accomplishment: "To date, we've delivered ten workshops, e-mailed nineteen weekly updates, and written forty new process flows." But, a better question than whether you are meeting your milestone goals is whether or not those goals are still relevant. Is the original reason behind the project still valid? Does your direction still squarely align with the current focus of the organization?

Remaining Agile

We want and even expect change to happen quickly, but this is not always the case. The bigger the organization, the slower the beast moves. Thus, when planning your timeline, do not be optimistic. Things almost always take longer than you think.

In the past, most people expected this. When a project completion date was set, experienced managers mentally pushed the date back. As the stated date drew near and it became apparent that the team would not meet the deadline, they would ask for an extension and, usually, be granted one. This happened all the time.

Years ago, there was more time to accomplish projects and more downtime between major change initiatives. In today's faster-paced environment, we do not have such luxuries. Change never stops. As such, we are forced to put in place the changes we can in the limited time allotted. Now, the practice is not to compromise on the milestone date but rather to compromise on the scope of the project. That is, many teams focus on what can be delivered with the timeline and resources available.

It is easier for people to accept a series of small changes rather than a major one. Focus on quickly implementing small steps over shorter time frames. Short, quick wins mitigate resistance because there is little to resist.

Asking for Help

As with any new business, when I first founded my consultancy I had to invest quite a lot of time in marketing my services to potential clients. Imagine, then, my delight at the first client who specifically sought me out and asked for my help. When I later asked her why she had done so, she said that when we had worked together on a Deloitte project, she liked that I questioned her decisions. She knew she did not have all the answers and welcomed input that would help her find better ones. In many cutthroat workplaces, there is little room to show that kind of vulnerability. Instead of admitting their uncertainty, many leaders feign confidence. They either knowingly make an uninformed decision or postpone making one altogether. Their natural instinct is to hide their lack of preparation and experience for the challenge as long as they can.

For the sake of your own success, you must be open about your need for help and advice. You may not need to publicly acknowledge your shortcomings in front of your entire company. You could turn to a select few for help. This could be your boss or a mentor. It could be a trusted peer or confidant.

You could even reach outside your company and find a coach or consultant. Regardless of where you decide to turn, seek help as soon as you realize you may not be up to a particular challenge. Just like you have to fill in the skill set gaps between your team members and their tasks, you must do the same for yourself.

The longer you go without addressing these shortcomings, the more obvious they will become. In some cases, they become so glaringly obvious that your superiors may have to step in to fix them. For instance, I worked with the president of a European company in the restructuring of his organization that necessarily involved layoffs. We worked with his executive team through a series of activities—workshops, grass-roots meetings, round-table discussions, and more—to clarify the common vision and enable those executives to return to London, Shanghai, Chicago and elsewhere to coach their local teams in preparing for the change.

Afterward, we conducted surveys to gauge the attitudes of the employees. Across Asia, the United Kingdom and North America, morale was generally high. With the labour laws of those countries, the transition from the old organizational structure to the new happened relatively quickly. The employees who remained after the layoffs knew what their new responsibilities were and felt secure in the continued stability of their positions.

The employees in France were another story. France's labour laws subject such organizational changes to a rigorous process. It involves renegotiating employee contracts, involving the local works council (the *Comité d'entreprise*) and more. In this case, the process was so extensive that the layoffs would have to occur over a period of two years, whereas in the United Kingdom, for example, they happened in two to three months. With such a lengthy period with looming layoffs, the French employees were insecure in their jobs. Without a clear career path ahead of them—that is, without knowing whether they would even have a job at the end of the year—the reorganization created a major disruption in their workflow and output.

But, this was not a case of being unprepared. We knew at the outset that the layoffs would happen over different periods according to the country. The hurdle was the vice president over France. Despite evidence to the contrary, he maintained that everything was under control. To hear his assessment of the change project, his region was on track to deliver exactly what was expected of him. Obviously, there was a mismatch between his perception and the reality.

Because the vice president was unable (or unwilling) to close that gap, the president himself had to step in to address the issue, much to the vice president's chagrin. Because the executive continued to pretend that everything was fine, the problem grew until it could no longer be ignored. Had he been more forthright about the challenges he faced, he could have received help early in the process. The president, the other vice presidents, or even I would have been happy to help. As it was, he had to be overruled and embarrassed in front of his boss and his peers.

Despite your best efforts, you will make mistakes. You will make a bad judgment call or realize in hindsight that you made the wrong decision. Failing to make the right decision does not mean that you are a failure. Your initiative will encounter setbacks, but that does not mean you should abandon the entire effort. Likewise, your decisions may lead to dead ends, but that does not mean you should declare yourself incompetent or incapable.

I explicitly state this because I have met many executives who were supremely confident in their own abilities only to see that confidence shattered when their entire project failed. While you want to plan for success, you must also be prepared for dealing with the opposite.

Do not wait to ask for help.

Challenge Questions

1. Have you and your team identified major risks and created contingency plans?
2. Have you identified substitutes for the key people in your project?
3. Does the structure of your project help you identify early warning signs of trouble?
4. In times of crisis, do you search for help to support you and to reduce your level of stress?

PHASE III

POPULATE

Delivering the Solution

By the end of the crusading phase, you are in the transition where your plan is being implemented. In crusading, your goal was to maintain the support of critical stakeholders, translate the vision of change into the required processes and adapt to new challenges as they arise. At this point, your circle of influence should encompass all representative stakeholders and at least 10% of directly affected personnel.

In the populating phase, the transformation is solidifying into the sustainable long-term processes and organizational structure that will ultimately deliver on the original promises of the initiative. But, to achieve this, you need to continue to ask the four key questions of why, who, what, and where:

■ *Why* am I populating?
To ensure individual acceptance of the new processes and structure

■ *Who* am I populating for?
All affected personnel

■ *What* am I populating for?
To solidify the new changes

■ *Where* will populating take me?
To delivery of the original expected results of the initiative

You need to achieve the buy-in of at least 80% of all stakeholders to fulfil the final goals of the initiative that will, in turn, deliver on the original strategy.

Chapter 9

Land Ho!

The future is not some place we are going, but one we create.

—John Schaar

"It's good to have you back, Monsieur Valery."

After his hospital stay and subsequent surgeries, the CFO [chief financial officer] had lost quite a bit of weight, making it seem like he had aged a few years in just a few months.

"Thank you. It's good to be back, although it's just until the end of the year. I wasn't planning on retiring this early, but my doctor and my wife have convinced me otherwise. But enough about me. Tell me about your big project."

"Well, as you know, we just scanned and paid the first invoice last week. So far, things have gone exceedingly well. After everything that it took to make it happen, I am not ready to believe everything is fine now."

"Well, you stayed right on budget and only went over the deadline by a couple of weeks. I think that's a success," Monsieur Valery said.

Mr. Schmidt nodded. "Anna and I both agreed that a failure would look bad for both of us. Me, for having been tasked with the responsibility in the first place, and her, for looking like she derailed what appeared to be a promising project. She threw her weight behind it, full force—including her contacts. That's how we found the Romanian company we settled on."

"I think it's a good choice. Do I remember correctly that I saw an e-mail saying you already have someone to liaise with the company?"

Mr. Schmidt nodded again. "Yes, surprisingly, one of my own accountants who was initially resistant to the whole project. But, he's excited about going down to Cluj once a month. He likes travelling and even has some distant relatives in Romania, so he jumped at the chance to be on site."

"Good, good. The senior executives are positive about the project. The CIO [chief information officer] even mentioned looking at trying to outsource IT [information technology] support again—provided you were part of the project. You may just become the resident outsourcing expert," the CFO said with a laugh.

Mr. Schmidt said, "It has been quite a race, but I'm glad it's coming to a finish."

Monsieur Valery turned serious. "Schmidt, let me offer you some cautionary advice. Things may be winding down, but the transformation is not over. Remember the IT department tried to reverse their outsourcing initiative just two months in. You need to solidify this. Don't rest on your laurels. Scanning your first invoice is a big milestone, but it is not the finish line."

Mr. Schmidt furrowed his brow. "That's a good point: Where exactly is the finish? When should I bow out and go back to my regular duties?"

His boss said, "My advice? Stay in touch with everyone you've worked with for at least a couple of months. Gauge their buy-in. Listen for problems. Lend a helping hand to anyone who needs it. This project is your baby, Schmidt—don't send it out into the cold, cruel world too early."

A few months after finishing a project with a client, I met one of the company's executives to follow up on the results. In the course of conversation, he jokingly said, "You know, we may need you to come back to help us with another project."

"Oh? Which one is that?" I asked.

"When you were working with us, had we begun the outsourcing project for accounts payable?" he asked.

"No, I don't believe so."

"Well," he said, "it's a disaster. The team in charge of the project didn't do a decent job of communicating the processes to the outsourcing company or training their people on how to handle our accounts. Basically, no invoices were paid for six months. It was so bad, the CEO [chief executive officer] had to personally guarantee that he would oversee immediate payment of back invoices for one of our major vendors so they would continue to supply us."

I will not reveal who this client is, of course, but let us say that if they built skyscrapers, then the supplier in question sold them the steel girders. This multimillion-euro company employing thousands of people would be forced to completely cease production.

The populating phase is not just about checking the boxes on your master plan. ("Seven transition workshops? Check. Employee survey completed? Check.") You must ensure that you have ultimately delivered the results that you originally promised to deliver. Obviously, if your CEO has to become personally involved to fix a problem, then you did not deliver the hoped-for solution.

If you come to this, the last phase, and you are not settling in to the new processes, then you still have much work to do. While the first two phases focus mainly on stakeholders and their buy-in, the populating phase is focused on deploying and delivering.

The Biggest Challenges in Populating

The biggest danger and challenge for a change leader during the populating phase is to be too self-confident, that is, too optimistic. You have been working for such a long time on building the new organization that you tend to assume that everyone has the same understanding as you and is equally motivated.

Although you will have an extended team of people working to explain the new responsibilities, to train people on the new processes, and to coach their colleagues in the new ways of working, it is critical to provide them with the tools and the structure they require. Your role in this phase of the change is really to support your extended team and guide them in their respective roles as agents of change. As they deploy and implement the new structures and processes, they may not be prepared to help others get on board. They may not be ready to be in the spotlight or to be questioned by their peers. They may need to learn how to be advocates of the change and to effectively interact with others affected by the change. Be sure you are available to support them and to step in if they need you.

Managing up is also a critical skill in the populating phase. As your initiative's visibility drastically increases, many executives may become anxious. They will begin to receive strong, unfiltered messages from their employees that will worry them. If you were effective in the mobilizing and crusading phases, this should be minimal. However, it is better to be safe than sorry: Proactively reach out to upper management to make sure they are still aligned and in sync with your efforts.

In the populating phase, the end is in sight. But, here in the last stretch, you must remain strong and resolute, adapting to the last-minute changes, keeping the initiative on track, and emerging as the leader your coalition needs you to be so that, together, you can make it to the finish line.

100% Buy-In?

As you see the end drawing near, you may wonder if you need 100% of affected employees to buy in to the new structure and processes. Luckily, the answer is no. Although 100% would be optimal, we must operate with the Pareto principle in mind. At the beginning of the mobilization phase, you need your sponsors' buy-in. Three to five key stakeholders actively supporting you with some resources should be enough for you to accomplish all that you need to in the mobilization phase. In the crusading phase, you should aim for about 10% of affected people to be on board. In the populating phase, your target is to have about 80% of all affected personnel working with the new processes and structures.

Reaching out to achieve at least 80% of the affected employees in a global firm with over 10,000 employees, for example, means that you cannot do it all by yourself. You must necessarily rely on your coalition and stock-standard change management tools such as employee workshops, side-by-side coaching, online forums, and standard training methods to ensure proper alignment between the knowledge, abilities, and processes of those affected by the change. Continued resistance may signal that those tools have not been as effective as they should have been.

If you did your homework during the crusading phase,

■ you will have an extended team of people in the different regions and departments ready and able to help you;
■ your extended team will have designed new processes that the different stakeholder groups will have reviewed and approved and will not be surprised to see in the populating phase;
■ you should not personally encounter major resistance in this phase of the project because now your extended team will be facing outward, toward the new employees to be brought on board.

What should you do with those who continue to actively or passively resist the changes? Some will eventually come around. I remember implementing new processes in a particular client's department. The manager and engineers resisted the new standardized approach. I faced strong pushback at nearly every local level: "This won't work for us. It doesn't match our needs. We want to continue working as we do now." But, of course, senior management had already made the decision, so we went ahead.

The funny thing is that ten years later, Acrasio was hired again to work with the same department and some of the very same people. We were replacing the then-current processes with a new centralized approach. Guess what we heard? "This won't work for us. It doesn't match our needs. We want to keep the approach we have now." That is, they wanted to keep the processes that they had completely rejected ten years earlier. In another ten years, when it comes time for yet another new approach, I do not wonder but that they will say the exact same things.

Resistance to change is a natural part of the journey. After about six months, most people will be so used to the new way of doing things that they barely even notice it anymore. However, some people will continue to resist, regardless of the circumstances. As long as you have the vast majority of stakeholders actively supporting the new vision and direction, though, the naysayers will be marginalized.

Although people certainly must take ownership for some of the on-boarding process, more often than not their lagging behind is the result of a failure in communication, training or planning.

Success Hinges on Communication

If you have read about change management from other sources, you might be surprised that until now, we have not spoken much about communication plans, training curriculum, different workshops, or other standard change management tools. Although these things are important and will help you deliver on your initiative, it is not your role to organize and deliver them. In your position, you should have experienced managers who can implement these tools on your behalf.

In the transitions I consult, we usually have at least three such delegates: a communication specialist, a change manager, and a training manager. Depending on the size of the organization, there can be more than one person fulfilling these functions. Based on their company knowledge, their experience in similar projects, and their personal skills, they will help implement the transition you have clarified and designed as the change leader.

When we plan the communication and training activities, we first identify the milestones and then design the different actions around them. After setting up a milestone-driven plan, we create the change architecture in which the different needs of the stakeholders are addressed. These types of things are the nitty-gritty of change management.

Your objective is to make sure that the key stakeholder groups and their needs have been identified, that you have a good structure in place, and that all affected employees have been identified and invited to join the transition.

The objective of good communication is to provide the basic facts, like the why of the change. You should not only highlight the advantages of the new approach but also explain why the old ways needed to be improved. Keep in mind that every individual naturally looks for the element of "what's in it for me." Although understanding the big vision would be key, everyone wants to understand how he or she is going to be personally affected.

But, communication goes beyond that. It is about setting the scene and creating positive emotions relating to the new ways. People will not accept information that is rosy yet misleading. They need to be emotionally touched to be willing to follow you on an unknown journey.

Communication is not only about conveying the relevant facts but also about conveying the relevant feelings.

Knowing You Have Arrived

You know you have largely arrived at your original goal when the ideas that were once supported by the few are now supported by the many, that is, once a broad contingent of the organization's employees and overall stakeholders has embraced the change and actively works toward its completion. At that point, you are no longer crusading a new idea. It has taken on a life of its own, gaining momentum on the shoulders of the masses, such that even if you were to halt your own efforts the change would continue.

But, just as the laws of physics dictate, that momentum can diminish over time. To continue into the long term, it must be codified in the internal processes of your company.

Next to communicating the why, do not forget to provide the how. People need to be told how to act, work and engage in the future. They do not need abstract theory but rather concrete examples with workflows, templates or even short videos. Depending on the level of change, they might also need to be trained on the new processes and skills.

Communication is not only the job of the communication manager. Your extended team will be the face of the changing business and, as such, your ambassadors. Equip them with communication packages, elevator pitches and brochures, but also support them in continuously interacting between the employees and yourself.

You will not be able to reach or convince everyone throughout your organization, but you can put in place elements to prepare about 80% of the affected people for the transition to come.

Measuring Success

How do you measure and recognize the quality of a deployment plan? First, your plan needs to be a good balance of a centralized approach (to reduce your costs) and customized delivery (to translate the change into meeting the needs of each specific stakeholder group).

Second, you should slowly build a story around the transition. For example, you would not want to shock the employees with a surprise invitation to trainings for a new system. Rather, you would build up expectation for the transition by slowly introducing the vision and then step by step laying out the understanding for the concrete individual changes required to achieve that vision.

Last, but not least, your plan should not mainly be measured on the delivery of different activities but rather on the delivery of the results. As discussed previously, meeting milestone goals and counting workshops is fine, but the most important thing is whether you arrive at the destination you sought. Only if you are able to achieve the concrete revenue targets or cost reduction will you have populated your organization with the new change.

Shades of Success

Depending on the scope of your initiative, the process of change can take months or even years to be finalized. You do not need to wait until the transformation is fully completed before you declare success. You could point to achieving your first deliverable, such as a measurable reduction in costs, the first new product off the line, the first sale of a new service or reaching other key indicators.

Those are tangible results you can point to, but the truth is that success is more about perception than reality. What I am about to say may be redundant, but the truth behind it is profound: The more that people perceive your initiative as a success, the more it will be a success. Achieving your goals is one thing; being perceived as a success is another. Although they are interrelated, they are by no means interchangeable.

Some people call this politics: Even though two people may achieve similar strategic goals, one is deemed successful while the other does not receive the same recognition. I can provide a perfect example. I once gave a presentation to a company group composed of both French and British executives. Afterward, one of the French executives approached me and said, "This was great. There was a lot of passion and emotional appeal in your speech. If all your communication is like this, I'm really looking forward to working with you. Great job." I graciously thanked him and went home feeling pleased with myself.

Then, I got a phone call from the client's CFO. He said, "Karin, the British have complained. They said that you didn't fully address their concerns. They wanted more facts and information. They felt your presentation was too theoretical and too high level."

There is a lesson in this about adjusting your communication to your audience's culture. But, the more relevant lesson here is that my efforts were considered an outstanding success by one group of executives and a dismal failure by another.

They were in the same room at the same time experiencing the same presentation, yet left with two different perceptions.

Some aspects of success are concrete, but success is largely about perception—from other people's points of view.

Challenge Questions

1. Are around 10% of the affected employees acting as your ambassadors and actively involved in deploying the change? Have you prepared them for their role?
2. Has the new structure—the organizational chart, policies, processes, and procedures—been firmly communicated and established?
3. Do you have a plan in place for training affected stakeholder groups in the new policies and procedures?
4. Are your key performance indicators in place to measure how successful you are in achieving your change objectives?
5. Are you able to end your involvement with the new structure continuing to function? Or, does it still require your participation?

Chapter 10

Captain's Log

What you get by achieving your goals is not as important as what you become by achieving your goals.

—Henry David Thoreau

"As much as I hate to admit it, Schmidt, I need some advice."

Mr. Schmidt grinned. "Well, Anna, for you to come to me, I know it must be bad."

As she sat down across from his desk, she said, "Although I did get some of the credit for how the A/P [accounts payable] outsourcing project turned out, you and I both know you did all the work. All I did was get out of your way."

"I disagree, Anna," he said. "You were opposed at the start, but in the end we created a genuine working relationship. Without your support and contacts, the project would have been a disaster."

She nodded. "Thank you, but my point is that, now that I've been tasked with outsourcing the accounting payroll, I don't know how to do what you did. After fighting with it, I am ... more appreciative of the challenges you faced. It isn't easy. People aren't backing me, my project team isn't doing what they're supposed to do, the HR [human resources] directors are upset about what it'll mean for them—it's quickly turning into a nightmare. I have to spend so much time babysitting people that I don't have any time to work on the project itself."

Mr. Schmidt smiled. "I wish I would have done what you're doing right now: asking for help before you get in too deep. I didn't, and it almost cost me my reputation in this company. Late in the game, I realized how little my pretty timelines and flow charts meant if no one else followed them. Fortunately, I had some talented people throughout the company who came forward to support me and then went out and sold the project for me—like you. If it hadn't been for them and you, the whole project would have collapsed."

Anna furrowed her brow. "So, what are you saying? I need to suck up to more people and leave the details to my minions?"

"No; I'm not saying either of those things. The details of your plan are important, but what's more important is getting real buy-in. If you're presenting real value to your bosses, your peers, your employees and your HR directors, there's no need to get people to like you—although that certainly helps. You earn their support by involving them, making sure their needs are met, addressing their concerns, and taking their perspectives into consideration. That is the first step toward them taking ownership of the change for themselves."

Seeing the sceptical look on her face, Mr. Schmidt said: "This is what I'm saying: don't manage projects—move people. You can accomplish more by inspiring change than by trying to drive it."

He paused and then said, "You see the name-plate on the door?"

Anna didn't turn around. "Yes. It says, 'CFO' [chief financial officer]. Don't remind me."

"Well, I'm sorry it's still a sore spot for you, but I need to make a point. I knew how to do Monsieur Valery's job before I was promoted, but I wasn't ready for his title until I learned how to effectively lead change. I had to embrace challenges and learn how to lead people before I finally earned the notice and respect of my superiors. The more challenges someone successfully takes on, the higher they can rise."

Anna bit her lip. "So, you're saying that leadership and buy-in are more important than assigning tasks and hitting deadlines."

Mr. Schmidt nodded. "That's what I'm saying."

She stood to leave. "Well, what I've been doing obviously hasn't worked. Let me think all this over. And don't you dare tell anybody I asked you for help."

"My lips are sealed."

She smiled and left.

He returned to the stack of papers in front of him outlining the new shared service plans. He had a list of people he would have to influence and persuade to obtain the resources and talent he needed to pull off the centralization effort. There was at least a year's worth of work ahead of him.

He took a breath, put on a smile, and reached for the phone.

━━━━━━━━━━━━━━━━━━

The corporate landscape is littered with failed initiatives at all levels and of all types of change projects that never broke even, much less provided any kind of return on investment. When AOL and Time Warner merged, they announced they would create the world's largest media company. By all accounts, the merger was a spectacular failure.

In an attempt to reduce the colossal costs of its Dreamliner aircraft, Boeing outsourced about 70% of its construction; the savings were more than offset by the redesign costs and delays.

Market initiatives, culture shifts, mergers, layoffs, pet projects—despite the differences in size, scope and specifics, the underlying theme among all of them is the same: A major corporate strategic initiative failed to deliver the hoped-for success.

Why do so many of these initiatives fail to live up to their expectations? At the outset, the proposed ideas seem promising. Companies usually have the resources and talent to successfully implement them. The payoff for doing so is often substantial—but it is not automatic. Change is not a destination, but a process.

Your life and career do not stop after you close out everything and declare success or failure. You will go on to new and different challenges, managing other people and resources and affecting the direction of other organizations. Before you go on, though, you need to stop to see what you took away from this one.

In Chapter 9, I presented the idea that success is subjective. The truth is that failure also is.

One time, I supported an information technology (IT) global outsourcing project. The collective opinion was that the outsourcing was a success, resulting in a 30% cost reduction with a comparable level of service support. Years later, though, I heard the company was preparing to reverse its decision and bring IT operations back in house.

You could look at the situation and say, "Oh, this is a step backward. Obviously, something was wrong because they're now rehiring their IT personnel. Did the project not work out like they planned? What happened?"

After I investigated a little, what I heard from the executives was that although the project had been a success from a cost perspective, the company had evolved. Instead of seeing

IT support as a cost centre, they had come to realize that it could be a key differentiator among the competition. By reinstituting the department, it could become a source of innovation in the company.

Again, from one point of view, it looks like they wasted their time outsourcing their IT department if, just a few years later, they reversed that decision. From the executives' point of view, though, the company had different needs at different times. They were adapting to their new perspective and new reality.

It is like winding a screw: It may look like it is just going in circles, but at the end of a turn, you have made real movement. The same can happen in your own change initiative: You may travel a circuitous route and come back to where you began, but you have personally made progress. You have learned, you have gained experience and insight, and you are a more valuable leader for the experience.

The Importance of Reflecting

It is important to reflect on your experience. In your own initiative, you may not have delivered the desired objective to change your organization. From the perspective of measurable results, you may have failed. But, if you learned some hard-earned lessons that you can carry into your next initiative, in that regard at least, your own experience was successful.

You may have helped other people grow and expand their skill sets. You might have helped the people on your implementation team pursue new opportunities. Perhaps working with them resulted in them becoming better professionals. Also, your new relationships within and without your organization carry forward with you into future projects. Do your sponsors and stakeholders recognize that a positive change occurred? Do new customers buy your products? It may be that you developed processes that allow the company to become leaner, faster or more efficient. From any of these perspectives, your experience was a success.

Successfully leading change begins with being an effective change leader. Before we even delved into Phase I, we addressed the five traits every executive needs to master before accepting an assignment. But, successful initiatives do not just begin with you as an effective leader—they also end with it.

Many successful entrepreneurs say that success is 50% hard work and 50% luck. This was certainly true for Mr. Schmidt. He pulled off his change initiative, but it was as much luck as it was skill. He was fortunate to have such supportive sponsors, a skilled implementation team, and an adaptive mindset.

Regardless of how your project turns out, you need to conduct your own personal evaluation. If a success, why did it turn out that way? Was it because of your efforts? Or, was it luck, like Mr. Schmidt's? If a failure, what could you have done differently?

Taking Personal Inventory

Molière said, "Nous ne sommes pas seulement responsables de ce que nous faisons, mais aussi de ce que nous ne faisons pas" ("We are not only responsible for what we do, but also for what we do not"). I rarely see change leaders stopping to reflect on what they experienced and learned.

Neither success nor failure is absolute. There are many ways to see and measure each. As a mature leader, it is your job to acknowledge the ways in which you brought about a positive change as well as the ways in which you failed to do so.

Even with the negative experiences, you can turn them into positive ones if you simply learn from your mistakes. I have seen acquaintances lose their jobs, devastating them. But, two or three years later, some of those same individuals are happier and more prosperous than ever before. In hindsight, being forced out of their comfortable job made them change and grow in unexpected ways that ultimately led to something better.

Instead of focussing on the results, refocus on what you are taking away from the experience. What lessons have you learned? What would you do differently if you had to do it all over again? Even if you had a positive outcome, where did you fail to adequately plan and to appropriately react?

You could perform this analysis immediately after the project is finished, but I suggest waiting three to four months. This gives you time to sit back, observe the effects, think about the experience, and contemplate the whole affair.

Better yet, your reflection on the experience and the lessons learned could be shared with the whole company. Reflecting and learning does not have to be an isolated experience. Rather, by making it a communal experience, everyone who participates becomes better at adapting and mastering change. This is especially important as your company moves forward. The more people there are with a pro-change perspective, the easier other such changes will be going forward.

I have conducted these types of "lessons learned" workshops for clients, but this is only one such vehicle for doing so. One client of ours developed a mentoring program by pairing experienced executives with managers undertaking a new change initiative—a system we enthusiastically encourage our other clients to copy. Also, by creating an explicit system (such as a knowledge management system) to transfer and disseminate experience, the institutional wisdom is not held by just a few veteran people at the top but dispersed throughout all levels of the company.

One day, the people who went through the change with you will be gone, but the need for change will always be there.

The End as the Beginning

The end of business change is the beginning of yet another change. A century ago, companies had the luxury of time. They could afford to make a slight adjustment or to end a major project, then sit back and wait to see what the effects would be.

Today, of course, such downtime is unthinkable. Nothing stands still that long. Economic pressure, new governmental regulations, client preferences, competitive innovations, internal turnover and other such forces collectively create a constant state of flux.

Yet, in the middle of such turmoil, change leaders like you must attempt to create structures and processes that endure. It is your responsibility to help your stakeholder groups find a way not only to change to the current set of proposed changes but also to learn to adapt to changes in the future. The end of one change project is just preparation for another.

Some people become overwhelmed at the thought of having to continuously change. That is one perspective. The more hopeful outlook, though, is that such constant challenges mean that you continuously have the opportunity to learn, to take on new obstacles, and to be constantly growing into an experienced change leader.

Whatever you experience, I hope you do not regret the opportunity you undertook. I hope you let it inspire you to attempt an even greater adventure.

Success is not a destination, but a journey.

Index

About the Author

Dr. Karin Stumpf consults for multinational companies implementing strategic change, such as DaimlerChrysler, Universal Pictures, Deutsche Bank, Bombardier Transportation, and the International Committee of the Red Cross. Formerly a consultant with McKinsey as well as Deloitte, she has worked with clients in more  than twenty countries to successfully support them in driving corporate strategy.

Dr. Stumpf regularly lectures in English, German, and French in venues such as the Swiss Institute of Technology, among others. She holds an MSc, an MBA, a PhD, and a master's in organizational psychology. Her consultancy, Acrasio, is based in Berlin, where she lives with her husband and daughter.